Employee Engagement
TAKING BUSINESS SUCCESS TO THE NEXT LEVEL

SHELDON D. GOLDSTEIN

NA

NorthAmerican
Business Press
Atlanta – Seattle – South Florida – Toronto

North American Business Press, Inc
Atlanta, Georgia
Seattle, Washington
South Florida
Toronto, Canada
Employee Engagement: Taking Business Success to the Next Level

ISBN: 9780988919372

Along with trade books for various business disciplines, the North
American Business Press also publishes a variety of academic-peer
reviewed journals.

Library of Congress Control Number: 2013948501
Library of Congress
Cataloging in Publication Division
101 Independence Ave., SE
Washington, DC 20540-4320
Printed in the United States of America
First Edition

CONTENTS

PREFACE

One of the valuable lessons we have learned in the past few decades is that having satisfied employees is not inconsistent with enjoying high profits. In fact it may be argued, as employee satisfaction increases, so does customer satisfaction and profit. Like pursuing quality initiatives, where managers see up-front cost looming large, encouraging dedication and loyalty amongst your employees may require an initial investment, but the benefits for the business in the longer term will more than pay for costs.

This book may be misinterpreted by some as a relinquishment of business authority by managers to employees who will act in self-serving ways. That is wrong. I do not recommend that the employees run the company, only that they should be integrated into the business organization as more than labor contributors. There are many different management styles that give rise to differing corporate cultures, all along the spectrum from highly autocratic (…"you're not paid to think, just do exactly as I say!") to completely consensual (…"we can't come to a decision unless we are all in agreement"). And, each of these cultures can result in successful businesses. However, the most successful outcomes are probably the result of some softening and consolidation of these cultures, where employees have an opportunity to voice their opinions and have input before final decisions are made by managers. As we will see, employees want to be a part of the decision-making process. While they don't need to have their opinions acted upon in every case, they need to be a valued part of the process.

When I started to write, I envisioned a series of essays I would give to my adult children as a guide through their work lives. Then I came to my senses and realized that they wouldn't pay any more attention to this advice than they have paid to any other advice I've given to them. I take comfort that this doesn't diminish the value of the advice, but rather speaks to the state of nature that is parenthood. Thus, the book format was conceived, but it has a new dimension and another dilemma. As a treatise for my children, it would be written from the perspective of the employee. However, the concepts of employee satisfaction relate to the cooperative efforts of employees and employers. Since we shouldn't consider employee satisfaction from a unilateral perspective, we must develop a framework where employees and their employers form a relationship. Furthermore, that relationship should transcend the structure of two groups (managers vs. employees) who have a coexistence that is sometimes uneasy, to a truly synergistic combination of interests and skills that add up to a total enterprise that is greater than the sum of the parts.

When employees are engaged by their employers and they become advocates for their companies, we have achieved our goal. This book is intended for employees to plan their employment strategies and for employers to structure the organization to meet the needs of all stakeholders, which includes building an environment that honors employees' needs and aspirations.

Sheldon D. Goldstein
Delray Beach, FL
2013

DEDICATION

To my grandchildren, Jake, Max, Noelle, and Lilley in the hope that they will have happy, productive, and successful careers.

CHAPTER 1: INTRODUCTION

"Organization doesn't really accomplish anything. Plans don't accomplish anything, either. Theories of management don't much matter. Endeavors succeed or fail because of the people involved. Only by attracting the best people will you accomplish great deeds." Colin Powell

Do you believe that employees are basically lazy? Is it your perception that for an employee to perform at acceptable levels, they must be scolded, enticed with slogans, paid bonuses, threatened with job loss, or made to do jobs as designed with as little thought or independent decision-making as possible to avoid the natural predisposition of employees to do as little as possible?

Or, do you believe that all employees are motivated and have good attitudes? Do you think that employees, if given the slightest encouragement, will perform at high levels because they would rather work hard and smart, and succeed, rather than be bored doing as little as possible?

Where we start our journey to achieve superior employee satisfaction depends on our vision of the workforce. Unfortunately, no two employees are alike, so we can't make generalized comments about anyone. However, as groups, employees can be motivated to high performance, and the higher the satisfaction level of our employees, the easier it is to achieve high performance and the higher the level of performance we can achieve.

As a message to employees who are reading this book to gain insights into recommended ways of demanding satisfaction from their employers according to their own definition, this is not going to meet your needs. Working cooperatively with your employer to meet the employer's needs will play an important part in your ability to enjoy a mutually beneficial relationship and a satisfying career.

As a message to managers and company executives who are considering not reading this book because they believe it is another lecture to give up their authority to employees or to satisfy employees' every whim in the interest of gaining "satisfaction points," that is not the intent of this book, either. It is the premise of this material that company executives and managers do the leading and employees do the transformation of raw materials into outputs, whether that is a product or a service. That does not mean leaders can't be informed by the employees, nor does it mean that every employee suggestion is the greatest idea since sliced bread.

While it is true that everyone can be motivated, not everyone can be motivated to do the work they were hired to perform. Some employees can be considered "poor fits" for the job, and the fact that they were hired and trained is perhaps a failure in the hiring process or the hiring manager. Generally, it is not the fault of the employee. This leads to the fact that employee turnover is inevitable, whether voluntary or the result of a discharge. It is the reason for employee turnover that is in question. There is an old adage that says employees hire into companies because they see potential for their personal and professional advancement, but they leave because of the people. Poor corporate policies, good policies inconsistently enforced, mean managers, unrealistic goals, poor communication, or low opportunity for learning and advancement are some of the reasons employees give for voluntarily separating from their employment.

Employees should be cautious when hiring into companies and employers should be mindful that some of their valuable employees leave for reasons that can be fixed easily and with little money.

CHAPTER 2: WHY EMPLOYEE SATISFACTION MATTERS

"Over 70% of people leave their jobs because of the way they are led." Norman Drummond

Happy employees make happy customers. But, more importantly, happy employees are productive.

The Business Case for High Employee Engagement

Unless improving employee engagement is good for the company and its shareholders, we shouldn't do it. This isn't all about the employees; it's about good business choices. If the employees happen to benefit, then this is a good venture, but our principle business is about profitability.

Some companies have a cultural direction and they are recognized for their focus. For instance, some companies concentrate their activities and investments on saving the environment. They take care that their mission and objectives are all aligned with this goal. And, there are certain mutual funds that cater to that sector. They hold shares in companies that adhere to environmental initiatives for investors who care very much about these issues. Similarly, some mutual funds may shun shares of companies that engage in tobacco, alcohol, or guns. And they cater to a sector of the investment community who care about avoiding shares of companies in these fields.

Then, there are companies that believe in the theory of employee satisfaction as a goal. They may apply for the "Best Places to Work" award in their state, or in the national competition. Their incentive is that winning this accolade is a noble achievement.

However, usually there is a benefit to the company that inures from concentrating on its employees. Happy employees tend to create happy customers. They stay around longer so the company has less attrition, less early retirement, and overall fewer turnovers. Happy employees are sick less often, improving productivity. Happy employees are more agreeable to be around; they are not always complaining about their jobs or bad-mouthing their company or coworkers. Companies that win employee satisfaction awards are often noticed by the press, which improves the company image. Improved company image is good for sales and leads to a surplus of prospective employees wanting to work for the company.

So, if we were able to concentrate on our employees' satisfaction as a primary goal and not worry about how much it costs, it is possible that we would enjoy all those peripheral benefits anyway, even if we really never cared about them. We'd accept them, for sure, but that is not the reason we paid attention to our employees' satisfaction. We did it because we care about our employees, and that's all that matters! It's not all that we get, but it's all that matters, until you start keeping score, at which point you realize that the benefits outweigh the costs.

Given these consequences of achieving high employee satisfaction, it is a surprise that more companies don't have a specific program to improve satisfaction. But, like quality efforts, many executives look at the up-front costs and fail to look at the longer-term returns.

Engagement Increases the Number of Customers

This benefit is the result of two factors. The first is that happy employees, those who are engaged, advocate for the company. This involves bringing friends to work at the company as well as signing up new customers. Second, happy employees speak well of the company whenever it is appropriate, and that entices customers to consider doing business with the company. It is the "word of mouth" advertising that is so effective.

Engagement Increases Customer Satisfaction and Loyalty

Happy employees are more gracious when working with customers. When customers experience a problem with a company's products or services and they are satisfied with the way the company handles aftermarket service, it makes them more loyal to the company than if the problem never occurred. This is because they have now experienced a little-used feature of the value package, and it worked well. In contrast, if they have never had an issue with a competitor's product or service, they don't know how well they will be treated given similar problems. Having that favorable Warranty experience works in your favor, and satisfied employees do this better than those who are not happy at work.

Engagement Reduces Cost

There are high costs associated with hiring and training employees. Good companies consider turnover of 5% to be on the high side, and if you are constantly hiring and retraining 5% of your payroll each year, the cost is outrageous. Depending on the level of hire, we can see costs of recruitment, on-boarding, training, and ramp-up from $10,000 to over $50,000 per employee, depending on relocation costs. Happy employees tend to stay with the company longer, thereby decreasing the cost of replacement.

Engagement Improves the Workplace Environment

Companies try to get employees to mingle in social situations. They have annual picnics, they organize bowling leagues and softball leagues, and they sponsor company outings at professional baseball games or other civic events. Working with someone outside of your employment environment on a charitable function for which you are both passionate creates a social bond. The theory is that employees who get along socially have a better work experience. It is harder to have a turf war with a coworker than it is to be cooperative with them at work when you are members of the same bowling team. You know them in a different setting and it is easier to like them. Under the social context, you are more likely to help them than fight with them.

We have all been in companies where some departments just seem to have more fun than others. They get together and have pitch-in lunches, they celebrate employee's birthdays, and they meet with each other on the weekends to go to the zoo or to a movie. It isn't an accident that this occurs in some departments and not others. It is an environment that is created by the boss or supported by the boss and created by some engaging members of the department. And people look forward to coming in to work in these departments much more than they like coming into work where there is no social interaction. If the company encourages a friendly workplace, then it benefits the company, the employees, and the customers, without costing the company a penny.

Engagement Is Good Press

Organizations are always trying to find a way to get favorable mention in the press. Being voted one of the "Top 100 Places to Work" is a way of being recognized as a superior employer. This list is published in local newspapers and some of the companies are interviewed by the press to highlight the factors that contributed to their success. Free advertising is always good when it spotlights a positive factor for the company.

Another factor that companies point to with pride is the average tenure of its employees. When employees stay with the company for a long time and average tenure is over 10 years, it is an indication that the company is a good place to work. This may often be measured by high levels and increasing trends in employee satisfaction metrics.

Engagement Supports Recruitment Efforts

Advocacy is a hallmark of engagement. Employees go from satisfaction to loyalty to engagement. Once engaged, their work lives don't seem like work anymore but rather another fun thing to do. They don't compartmentalize their day to be work vs. personal time as much, and they see their employment as an important and desirable part of their lives. When so engaged, it is natural for them to recommend their employer to friends and acquaintances. Many employees hate their jobs and wouldn't think of telling their friends about a job opening, but advocates do just the opposite. If they know of a job posting at work they approach talented friends and acquaintances to recommend them to the job. They are proud of their employment and proactively share their workplace as a desirable place to work.

End Note

There have been many studies that show superior business results accrue to companies that follow the tenets of the Baldrige Criteria and whose executives practice empathetic leadership. In his book on "Emotional Intelligence," Goleman studied the business results of several companies that were adversely affected by the 9/11 attacks on the World Trade Center. His work followed the impact of the disruption to the companies' businesses for a few years after the horrible loss of life and resulting loss of human contributions to the firms. In those companies where the leader practiced caring for the families of those who were lost, regardless of the cost to the company, those companies rebounded more quickly and profitably than those organizations that were more interested in getting back to "business as usual."

CHAPTER 3:
WHAT DO EMPLOYEES WANT?

"Never tell people how to do things. Tell them what to do and they will surprise you with their ingenuity." George Patton

Some employees want a job while others want a career. This may be linked to the corporate culture, but it may not. Some employees do not define their lives by their jobs. A job is merely a means to make enough money to live a reasonable life, as they define it. Some employees have simple needs that are easily met with the pay from mid-level jobs that they perceive as secure, if they perform at an acceptable level. They don't want a lot of responsibility, nor do they want to manage others. Just give them work that they are trained to do, and they are happy. No overtime, cross-training, job enrichment, promotions, and no stress. It is not that they don't want to do excellent work, and they definitely feel pride in accomplishment. Their goal is to keep work in a comfortable place in the structure of their lives, and it doesn't have the highest priority.

Other employees have more complicated or expensive dreams that require higher level jobs. These employees want a career, and more importantly, they want a career path. They may be no more dedicated than those who want a job, but a system that can meet their needs differs from a system that meets the needs of the job seeker.

In fact, a company will have a mix of each of these employees, and both types need to be accommodated by the corporate culture as well as honored by the management team. Other than the need for job enrichment and promotion opportunities, our two types of employees need very similar attributes from their employer.

Generational Factors

On this same note, we have employees who fall into different generations and their needs tend to be driven by the generation in which they were born. In statistics, we call this "bins." In statistical theory a bin is a grouping of data (objects or people fall in this category) that have some characteristics in common.

Bins

Schools create bins when we grade course performance. Excluding +'s and -'s, a grade between 70 and 79.99 is a "C" and a grade between 80 and 89.99 is a "B." These are bins of performance where students whose grades fall in those numerical categories are given the same grade.

Some time ago I ran a company and we decided to market our products and services on the radio. The marketing reps who came to see me about advertising asked me what radio station I listened to. Unfortunately, I did not listen to their stations. When I told the reps what station I listened to generally, their comment was that my choice was strange since "that station is geared to women between the ages of 18 and 35." Without divulging too much about my profile, I do not fall in that category, and their statement explained quite a bit about the content of the station.

However, what was clear is that radio stations specialize content to attract certain demographics. Women between the ages of 18 and 35 like to listen to a specific type of music, hear similar banter between the radio personalities, engage in certain call-in games, and they are interested in similar products and services. In short, everything about that station's programming in that time slot is intended to cater to the 18 to 35 year old women. This is a bin. It is defined by a group that has similar characteristics.

The Generations

The most common generations in the workforce today are the Baby Boomers, Gen Xers, and Millennials. They each have different characteristics and they are motivated by different drivers. So, as we review methods to motivate employees we must be keenly aware that a "one size fits all" approach will not work with our different generations of employees.

As a simple digression, in a survey of customers I conducted for a service company, one of the question options was "How important is 24 hour service?" The answer required customers to rank the three most important attributes and the three least important attributes where "24 hour service" was a choice. In the survey results, 24 hour service always came up in the three most wanted responses. Strangely, 24 hour service also came up on the least important lists. This was a conundrum until I called some of the customers and discovered that our customer base was split into two main groups on this question. There were many customers who absolutely needed 24 hour service and an equal number who didn't; in fact they preferred to be scheduled for first call the next day. These are bins for that characteristic and they need different solutions for their service needs.

The following information is taken from a summary of two sessions at the 2008 International Lilly Conference on College Teaching. It highlights the characteristics of our employees based on their birth generations.

Characteristics of the Most Common Generations in the Workplace		
	Baby Boomers (**Born 1946 – 1964**)	**Gen Xers** (**Born 1965 – 1981**)	**Millennials** (**Born 1982 – 2002**)
Values	Recognition, enthusiasm	Technology, skill development	Convenience, connections, community
Traits	Optimistic, idealistic, competitive, question authority, workaholics	Independent, self-reliant, skeptical, resourceful, adaptive, distrustful of institutions	Optimistic, hopeful, confident, respect for–not awe of–authority, globally concerned, multitaskers
Feedback	Give feedback to others, but rarely receive it	Need immediate and honest (positive) feedback	Seek constant (immediate) flow of communication
Reputation	Self-absorbed, workaholics, fickle, rigid, hypocritical, and impractical	Cynical, ungrateful, disloyal, overly casual, not team players, undisciplined	Inexperienced, overly confident, impatient, lazy, naïve, overly influenced by pop culture
View of College	A cultural "experience"	An investment	A work requirement

A note about this table is in order. Obviously, not all employees who fall in each age group act in exactly these ways. These are generalizations, however knowing this information may help managers understand the underlying motivations and actions of their employees and why they want what they ask for.

Motivation

How should we motivate employees? What makes employees motivated?

This chapter is not intended to cover the many motivational theories related to employee satisfaction and productive capacity. Suffice it to say that a summary of some concepts will convey the basic process we should consider when putting in place an organizational structure that encourages employees to perform at high levels and supports their interests through work rules. Employees will tell us which work rules maximize their willingness to perform at world-class levels.

We can easily get bogged-down thinking that employees will always be self-serving in their "needs." This leads us to the conclusion that given empowerment to decide how to structure their work environment, this will always result in lazy behavior and low productivity. However, let me assure you that there is no conflict between employee empowerment, satisfaction, and company performance at a high level. They may all coexist in harmony, and in our context of developing a system to promote employee satisfaction, they usually will. So, where did this notion of "lazy" employees come from?

McGregor's Theory "X" and Theory "Y" Employees

Back in the 1960's, McGregor at MIT's Sloan School of Management developed his "Theory 'X' and Theory 'Y'" vision of employee management. In essence:

Theory "X" employees generally:

- Dislike work
- Are motivated principally by threats and coercion
- Will avoid responsibility whenever they can
- Need a structured work environment with narrow scope of authority

Theory "Y" employees generally:

- Enjoy work
- Are committed to company goals
- Accept responsibility

- Have the intellectual potential to willingly engage in creative problem-solving

These concepts of employees' basic motivations in the workplace often lead managers (depending on their conviction of which theory prevails) to assume a management style that will be most effective in managing their employees. This means that each manager has a predisposition to believe that employees, all employees, generally fall into either Theory "X" or Theory "Y" behaviors.

However, a misconception about Theory "X" and Theory "Y" is that they represent two extremes of the behaviors and beliefs of employees. Therefore, *good* employees are more like Theory "Y" people, and *bad* employees behave like those described as Theory "X" people. Rather, both theories may be in play for any employee at any time. There is a spectrum of needs that employees have that may depend on the task they have to do (not one of us really enjoys every task we have to perform on our jobs to the same degree). Also, some people really enjoy their jobs, but don't want much responsibility. While no employee perfectly fits the mold of all the behaviors identified by McGregor in each category, we can appreciate the general trend.

Herzberg's Two-Factor Theory

Frederick Herzberg engaged in motivational research beginning in the 1950's. His Two-Factor theory postulates that there are factors in an employee's work life that lead to satisfaction, and there are factors that lead to dissatisfaction. An interesting side note is that satisfaction and dissatisfaction are not opposites.

In fact, Herzberg's theory claims that satisfaction is related to:

- Achievement
- Recognition
- The work itself
- Responsibility
- Advancement
- Growth

And, dissatisfaction is related to:

- Company policies
- Working relationship with your boss
- Supervisor's style
- Work environment
- Salary
- Relationship with your peers
- Feelings of security

Herzberg called satisfiers, 'motivators' and called dissatisfiers, 'hygiene factors.' The motivators are aligned with the conditions of the job. Hygiene factors are aligned with working conditions.

Therefore, since there are different factors that influence satisfaction and dissatisfaction, there are two different scales we should use.

No Satisfaction…………………………………………………….……Satisfaction

Dissatisfaction……………………………………………………...No Dissatisfaction

We can point to several conclusions from this theory. First, salary is mainly related to dissatisfaction. In other words, salary is not a motivator, but the absence of a competitive salary is a dissatisfier. Having a competitive salary would represent no dissatisfaction. So, if you really want to satisfy an employee, you should concentrate on the motivating conditions such as recognition and advancement, among the others on the list. Second, if we measure employee satisfaction, we will not be able to ascertain dissatisfiers as a lack of satisfaction. In other words, if employees say they are not satisfied with their level of responsibility, that doesn't mean they are dissatisfied with the attribute. It only means they are not satisfied, since dissatisfaction is on another scale entirely.

For this reason, as we look in the Baldrige Criteria in Category 5: Workforce Focus, we will find questions that relate to both satisfiers and dissatisfiers (motivators and hygiene factors) to establish an overall view of both scales that affect workforce engagement.

While there are critics of each theory, they have formed the basis of motivational programs for decades.

Motivation Drivers

Let's say that a competitor targeted one of your employees with a job offer that beat the salary they are paid at your company. How many of your employees would be able to respond like this?

"I'm flattered by this invitation, but …… I'm not interested in an opportunity with your company. Here, my manager treats me with respect, I am acknowledged for doing a good job, I am given all the resources and support I need to do a good job. My job is being improved because I told my manager ways I think it would work better and in ways that improve my ability to help the company and the customers at higher levels. I am paid fairly, and I have good benefits. My manager and employer understand my need to have balance in my life, and they encourage me to pursue outside interests that include my family, because they know that when I am needed to give the extra effort occasionally, I will step up for the company. I am informed about how my contribution affects our customers, and I'm informed about how the company is doing. That helps me understand how I am progressing in the job. I've been here over 5 years, and I like my coworkers. So, given that, what can you offer to me that is better than what has already been demonstrated by my current employer? I'd be taking a big chance going with you!"

Probably not too many of your employees will respond that way. Did you notice that money was not that important an item on the list of attributes desired by this fictitious employee? In fact, while managers believe that compensation is the number one motivator of employees …"one research study found that the top five employee needs in the workplace are":

- Interesting work
- Recognition
- Feeling "in" on things
- Security, and
- Pay

Reference The Management and Control of Quality, 6th Ed., Ch. 6, p. 273, Evans and Lindsay, 2005, Thomson Southwestern

Note that pay shows up in the list of top five motivators, but we showed that in the Hertzberg theory, pay is a hygiene factor. My conclusion to this apparent dilemma is that if a company does not have a competitive pay scale, it will show up as a motivator, but once the pay is competitive, it shows up as a hygiene factor.

To be sure, some employees will jump ship for $0.25 an hour increase in pay. It is my experience that employees who show that lack of loyalty are either paid at very low levels such that a small increase in pay has real meaning to them, or they are actually unhappy on the job and would have switched for any reason. They are caught in a trap because they are not viewed as important enough to the company, and losing them is not a costly affair. They are considered commodities in the marketplace, easily replaced at minimal cost. Many companies have employees who are treated that way.

Who are the valuable employees? Most companies concentrate their attention and rewards on the top 5%–10% of their performers. The rest are commodities.

All About Engagement

What makes employees engaged? Since each employee is an individual with their own specific needs, this is a complicated question. We can't do everything that every employee asks, because that is impractical. So, what does the literature say works to achieve high employee engagement?

Let's start out with a description of what is not employee engagement. Some companies address employee engagement as if it is defined as the way the company reaches out to employees to "engage" them with benefits, training, or social interactions. Their interpretation is to engage with employees by holding Town Hall meetings where there is personal interaction between the company's management team and the employees. However, that is not what employee engagement means in the hierarchy of employee satisfaction/loyalty/engagement. What we mean in this context is that employees show a desire to perform at high levels because it is satisfying to do it and it makes them feel a sense of personal accomplishment and pride.

When companies spend time concentrating on the benefits to the company that accrue from their efforts to improve employee engagement and not enough time engaging employees because it is the right thing to do for their workforce, then they are doing it for the wrong reasons, and those reasons will be transparent to the employees. When the efforts appear to be more in the best interests of the company, and the benefits to the employees are simply a vehicle to get there, it is perceived as disingenuous, and it will fail. This is not to say that there won't be substantial benefits to the company by selflessly concentrating on employees. But, those company rewards have to arrive as a side benefit and not be the focal point of the process.

An example I have found with students in a college degree program provides a parallel. Students who come to class to learn the material and receive the best education they can are usually rewarded with good grades. Their motivation is to get smarter and improve their lives. Alternatively, students who come to class to get good grades, regardless of how much they learn, often don't do as well with their grades and don't learn as much. Their motivation is to "check the box" and get the course behind them with a good grade. Since that is the driving force, they try to outguess the instructor on what will be on the exams and quizzes, studying only that material. Their concentration is on the grade and not on the learning. They learn a bit in a limited sphere; and if they guessed wrong and studied the wrong material, they do poorly on the exams. In this scenario, they don't learn much and they don't get that good grade either.

Similarly, companies that concentrate on employee engagement receive good customer satisfaction and financial results. Those that concentrate on doing just enough to "get good employee satisfaction scores" as long as it contributes to profit, might miss out on the engagement and therefore miss out on the broader benefits of higher customer satisfaction, lower absenteeism, and higher employee retention.

Some Selected Studies

In the text "Human Resource Management", 13th. Ed., 2013, Pearson Education, Inc., it is reported that "The Institute for Corporate Productivity defines engaged employees 'as those who are mentally and emotionally invested in their work and in contributing to an employer's success'." This measure of success may be recognized as higher profit margins enjoyed by the employers of engaged workers. Among other comments in this text, a survey by the Gallup organization said the "business units with the highest levels of employee engagement have an 83% chance of performing above the company median, while those with the lowest employee engagement have only a 17% chance of performing better than the company median."

"A survey by consultants Watson Wyatt Worldwide concluded that companies with highly engaged employees have 26% higher revenue per employee."

In an article in the Harvard Business Review: ... "when it comes to customer service, satisfied employees aren't enough. Instead, 'Employees should be engaged by providing them with reasons and methods to satisfy customers and then rewarded for appropriate behavior'."

A Towers Perrin document Working Today: Understanding What Drives Employee Engagement indicates that "Engagement-supporting actions include making sure employees (1) understand how their departments contribute to the company's success, (2) see how their own efforts contribute to achieving the company's goals, and (3) get a sense of accomplishment from working at the firm."

The HR management consulting firm Mercer "found that as of 2010, employers planned to focus both on money and on career development to retain and engage the right talent…rather than focusing on incentives and perks to entice and retain employees, organizations …will hold onto the most talented workers…by offering them a range of professional experiences, broad functional and geographic exposure within the organization and more targeted leadership opportunities…as part of the employer's total rewards package."

There have been quite a few studies into the root cause of employee engagement. None of them focus on pay. Here are some snippets that will give us an idea of the scope of inducements that have been shown to work.

Upward Career Opportunities

In a study by Right Management, "Global Benchmarking Study," December 2009, of 28,810 global employees, published in the January 2011 issue of Quality Progress, employees are asked to agree or disagree with the question "There are career opportunities for me at my organization." Those respondents who report that their employer provided favorable career opportunities scored engagement rates of 54%, while 46% reported that they are not engaged.

For those employees who believed that there are unfavorable conditions for career opportunities, 9% reported that they are engaged, versus 91% who were not engaged. While it clearly takes more than career opportunities to get employees engaged in their jobs and with their employers, when employees feel that there is a lack of upward mobility for their careers, they are very disengaged. They are in a holding pattern until a better opportunity comes along at another employer.

Other Factors

Drivers of satisfaction and dissatisfaction are covered in other chapters. Now, let's look at the drivers of effectiveness. It comes as no surprise that these are operational objectives, such as clearly communicated directives, access to information and resources, and authority to make decisions. So, what about engagement?

In an article from EzineArticles.com, Juan Riboldi also states that the "discretionary effort given by employees" is motivated by such factors as:

- Fit with strengths
- Values alignment, and
- Stimulating work environment and teams

I call these the "if it were my company, I'd do it this way also" factors. This recognizes that not all employees are good fits with a company regardless of their technical abilities alone.

The values of the company should be the same values held by the employee. As an example, let's say a company believes strongly that they will obey the letter of the law that governs its operations and go no further. "We're not interested in the spirit of the law as long as ignoring the spirit of the law won't result in any negative financial consequences to us." If an employee can't be comfortable working in that environment, then they should not seek employment here. If a company has routine fundraisers (say by permitting employees to wear jeans for $3 a day), and then they contribute the money to an organization that isn't respected by an employee, then the employee might consider whether their values align with the company, either because of the pay-for-play nature of casual wear or the specific recipient of the donation.

Nothing curbs enthusiasm more quickly than a work environment and coworkers that sap your creativity and momentum. Picture a workplace that continuously encourages new ideas and a team of coworkers who are fun to work with because they contribute in constructive ways and view your success as a success for the entire team. It sounds idyllic, but if you look at the profiles of the "100 Best Companies to Work For," those are the characteristics we see.

- Employees may be given 4 hours a week to pursue any projects they think are useful,
- Work groups that are trained to be effective,
- Authority to make decisions without layers of management approval

These are some of the benefits that add up to a stimulating work environment.

There are another two motivators that figure into the formula. One is obvious and the other not so much.

The one that is not quite so obvious is that Riboldi states accountability is a motivating factor in driving engagement. This is not necessarily intuitive. Don't employees want "no" accountability? If we subscribe to the theory that employees want responsibility to conduct their jobs in their own ways, then accountability comes along with that responsibility.

The obvious one is that great leadership is a motivator of engagement. This is also reflected in an article in the Human Resource Executive in their Jan/Feb 2012 issue by J. Wiley of Kenexa's High Performance Institute. He states that the #1 "driver of engagement is senior leaders who inspire confidence in the future." This is clearly a trait of great leadership. "I think people appreciate being talked to honestly and openly about the state of the business, but ultimately they've got to have confidence that leaders in the organization have a vision and can find a way forward."

In one study by the Gallup organization, the poll reports that "just 28% of employees are 'engaged,' characterizing the rest as 'not engaged' or 'actively disengaged'." In another study, the key components of a successful employee engagement strategy are:

- Vision and strategy
- Alignment of work and personal skills, and
- Management support

Another study indicated that the drivers of employee engagement are:

- Reduced role conflict
- Proper training
- Personal autonomy

In other words, *satisfaction* is driven more by competitive pay, benefits, and an empathetic boss; but *engagement* is the result of a great leader who pulls employees into the mission of the company and creates an environment where employees are challenged and supported to do great work with high levels of autonomy.

In an article in the Wall Street Journal, September 16, 2009, Business Owners were shown to have the highest level of happiness and well-being. The reason is that being the boss and having autonomy in their daily work lives promotes contentment and "emotional and physical health." The top three professionals for well-being are, Business Owner, Professional (such as doctor or lawyer), and Manager/Executive. Those occupations that fall at the bottom of the well-being scale represent jobs that have decided lack of control, participation in decision-making, and hectic and/or repetitive tasks, such as transportation or manufacturing jobs.

The elements that comprise engagement motivators may be called the "culture" of the organization. They arise from the top of the company and are:

- Driven by the CEO
- Hard to change, and when change is affected by a new management team, they take a long time to change
- Difficult to quantify in statistical terms
- Required in different combinations of elements for different employees

Why would an improvement in culture be difficult to change? The reason is, change is often resisted because some employees liked the old way, or some employees are skeptical of the motives behind the change, or the benefit to the employee arising from the change is not made clear.

In addition, each employee has different needs. Some employees would appreciate an in-house daycare facility while others value a free lunch more. As long as the company provides something for everyone, then it can work to improve engagement. For those employees who are not motivated by any of the cultural elements, they should probably find another job.

Employers Need Objective Systems

When an organization is evaluated for performance, we have already discussed the need for documented systems. When we look at the Baldrige Category 5 requirements, how can we display that we have a fully developed system of processes intended to improve employee satisfaction? What are the specific requirements for management to consider? Let's list some of these requirements:

- Assess workforce capability and capacity needs
- Recruit, hire, place, and retain new workforce members
- Organize and manage your workforce
- Improve workforce health and security and workplace accessibility
- Ensure workforce continuity and prevent workforce reductions
- Foster a culture of open communication, high-performance work
- Support high-performance work and intelligent risk taking
- Consider compensation, reward, recognition, and incentive
- Assessment of workforce engagement, retention, absenteeism, and grievances
- Relate engagement to key business results
- Learning and development system focus on ethics, performance improvement, core competencies, and knowledge transfer from departing employees
- Career progression

In order to be credible, any system must have a well-developed process of learning, implementation, surveying, improvement, and results. It is one thing to say it in a mission or vision statement and another thing completely to demonstrate that you are living to that standard.

When we look at companies known for being employee-friendly, what we find is that they ask employees what they need to make their work environment conducive to high performance and what they need to make the workplace a comfortable destination. In other words, they ask their employees for advice.

The second attribute is that the employer takes action to improve the environment in ways that are most important to the employees while still being consistent with their corporate mission.

The next step is to ask employees if the actions taken were those that the employees wanted, and if there were any issues with the implementation.

And lastly, the employer correlates the changes to company results. These results may be increased productivity, lower absenteeism, higher rates of retention, increased customer satisfaction, or improved employee satisfaction and engagement, to name a few.

So let's go through these and see what would be an appropriate process to display that convincingly proves we are taking these issues seriously.

- Assess workforce capability and capacity needs, and
- Prepare your workforce for changing capability and capacity needs, prevent workforce reductions, and prepare for growth

It seems that every time a new CEO is hired in a company, he or she trims down the organization. They sell divisions or let go of people. How do companies get so bloated with employees that aren't needed? The answer is that companies fail to take assessment of the workforce seriously, and they fail to manage the workforce needs of the company and its talent mix with the changing business environment. It seems that we always know when it is time to hire more people, but trimming the workforce or changing the mix of skills is not always in clear focus. If we had a better handle on this, we might be able to do more downsizing based on retirement or losing people through attrition than with firings or layoffs. If we paid more attention to our dynamic workforce issues, it would be easier to meet our current needs because we planned for it rather than having to do it as a fire drill.

How would a company demonstrate that they assess workforce capability and capacity on a routine basis? A great way to show this is to have a process that engages each department manager with HR to coordinate training activities and hiring plans with marketing projections. This would be a formal meeting with recommendations and action items. At any time we could see how the company was performing according to those plans.

Recruit, hire, place, and retain new members of your workforce to meet your current needs.

This requires a plan to find and keep employees. Once we hire an employee, it is expensive and time consuming to replace them. If we can show that there is a systematic process in place to write job descriptions, place ads in media that will attract employees of diverse backgrounds, bring in employees with a well-defined on-boarding process, and develop employees so they have ever-increasing opportunity in the organization, that would be a good start.

Is there a defined hiring process with interviews conducted by several people in the organization? Do all employees have to pass a skills test or another qualifying test? Is this consistent among all employees for particular jobs? Do the hiring requirements vary to meet the needs of jobs that require different skill sets?

Many companies have very informal on-boarding procedures. There is the usual paperwork to fill out for HR, the 401k plan to enroll in, tax forms must be completed, and the employee is shown to their desk. Some companies take it a step further and introduce the new employee to their colleagues and review the general job objectives. But how many companies review the organization chart with new employees? Offer new employees a training program on the most useful company forms that are required for travel vouchers, expense reports, capital requests, or office supplies? Should a new employee be introduced to those other department personnel with whom they will interact? Depending on the job, if there is a fixed process that an employee must follow, such as a call center or a service desk, all new employees should go through a training session before being placed on the phones to shadow an experienced employee. The idea is to set up the new employee for success through thorough training and not simply trial by fire. In many positions there are regulatory requirements as well as company policy that must be followed, or it places the company in jeopardy. Telling an employee about these rules isn't the same as training them in the rules. It is harder to document that something was communicated than it is to show that formal training has occurred.

Organize and manage your workforce

There are several parts to this question. It asks whether there is a plan for organizing the workforce. Are there departments; is there a process for project management; is there a matrix organization that is utilized to tackle major projects; who coordinates the work of the organization; and how are they held accountable for results? Is there a sense of what the organization's strengths are, and are they leveraged for success? Is the process focused on customers, and is there a concentration of exceeding performance expectations? In other words, what is the documented process for managing your workforce that ensures results and manages employees to achieve superior results for the company? Saying, "sure, we do that," isn't enough. There has to be documented evidence that it occurs on a routine basis.

Improve workforce health, safety, and security for different workforce groups

This requirement relates to two very important factors for employers to consider. The first is that there has to be documented and repeatable implementation of an improvement program for employee health, safety, and security. Even if results are fine, there should be an ongoing plan and program to continuously improve this important aspect of your employees' work. The second is recognition that different employees should be treated differently. In other words, one size doesn't fit all in many cases. Segmenting employees into groups that tend to be driven by the same motivators indicates that employers understand the varying needs of office personnel versus field personnel, to give an example.

The way we close the loop on continuous improvement is to survey our employees after effecting a change to see if the change had the desired result. In fact, when we report our results for the period, we should indicate what our measures and goals were when we started our improvement process; and, after polling the results of employee surveys, we have achieved xx% of the goal, and that compares (un)favorably with the results of past performance and also compares (un)favorably with results of our competitors/industry/benchmark standards. Only when we can show results are we demonstrating that there is more than a process; we are showing that the process is effective.

Determine the key elements that affect workforce engagement and satisfaction for different workforce groups and segments

The "one size fits all" method of employee satisfaction is challenged in this requirement. The employer is asked to determine what elements of the environment support employee engagement but also to customize those elements for different work groups or segments. This can be broken up by division, by state, by department, or by salary class; but there has to be a method to assess engagement for these different groups, which means segmenting the data and then customizing engagement programs for each identifiable segment. When the process is audited, the data that is important will be the independent results for each segment and how it was obtained.

Foster a culture of open communication, high-performance work

People work better in an environment where there is cooperation. One of the reasons offered for open work spaces (office locations without walls, where employees have open access to each other by line-of-sight as well as uninhibited voice communication) was the ability to gain information quickly and informally. The idea is to promote open communication and support for the team. It may be argued that in today's culture of information accessibility via electronic media, the disadvantage of open work spaces (which results in a total lack of personal privacy) takes on a higher cost. However, a work environment that promotes helpfulness also promotes high performance in a work group.

The willingness to be helpful transcends the physical workplace. In companies that promote helpfulness, it is the people who do it, not some policy. People are hired because they can work well with others. It is often said that it is incredible what can be done if we don't care who gets the credit. Well, when we hire employees who are cooperative and can work well in teams, we find that they support each other. They are enervated by the success of the team, and this is their reward. Personal success is not their main goal; it is the performance of the team that is recognized and rewarded. The company can set up employees to be mentored or to work in groups that are judged by the output of the team's efforts, but ultimately it is the hiring of employees whose egos are comfortable contributing in a team environment and who enjoy helping others where open communication will thrive.

Some questions we can ask are:

1. How does the company identify office politics?
2. How are information barriers eliminated?
3. Are there new processes that can be instituted to improve knowledge transfer more quickly and efficiently?
4. How do you know?
5. What did you do to foster it?
6. What was the result?
7. How did the employees react to your changes?
8. What was the employees' feedback about the improvement?
9. How did the improvements correlate to improvements in your business?

As is typical with these questions, unless we have a system in place to measure our responses to these questions and have definitive answers based on survey results and action items, we cannot demonstrate that we are really doing it. Nothing trumps documentation.

Support high-performance work

Now that employees are given an environment to engage in high performance work, when they need resources to accomplish that task, are those resources available? Can an employee spend money to support their work? This category differs from the one we just considered because the last topic refers to the company creating an environment for high performance work. This topic speaks to the ability of the employee to individually request resources to accomplish their work and the likelihood that the company will make those resources available to them.

How much of a budget is given to each department for discretionary spending? How is the budget established? Who has authority to spend the budget?

What is the process to quickly evaluate an employee request and provide the support needed for high performance work?

Consider compensation, reward, recognition, and incentive

What are the factors that impact an employee's compensation? When we reward an employee for doing a good job, we should consider non-cash awards as quite valuable. This reminds me of the story of the golden banana. One version has its origin many years ago at Hewlett-Packard when an engineer burst into his boss' office to announce a breakthrough in a long-standing problem. The boss was so overcome with delight that he quickly glanced around his office to find a token of appreciation, and finding none, he took a banana out of his lunch bag and handed it to the incredulous employee with his hearty congratulations. By another account, over the years that award became a lapel pin and was awarded to only one employee each year. It was the most prestigious award the company conferred, and instantly recognized as a badge of honor by all employees.

Regardless of the facts surrounding this award's beginnings or its final manifestation, the idea is to find ways to recognize employees in both monetary and non-compensatory ways. Employee of the month awards can be motivational as well as many other ways the employer can show appreciation for employee contributions. Sometimes the non-monetary rewards are the most coveted. If the company has a documented process to ask employees what is the most important contribution they can make to support the company's mission, and then they reward employees for accomplishing specific, measurable goals in that area, they are taking a giant step toward recognizing employees in ways that are most important to them.

This process can be taken to extreme. In one company I know, a manager would send out sticky posts to employees whenever there was a hint of a positive vibe. Some employees had dozens and dozens of her sticky notes, making them ridiculous. They would post them on their computer monitor as recognition of the frivolous nature of the "award." To convey the correct level of importance, it must be rare, link directly to a valued accomplishment, and be easily recognizable to every employee who sees it. When you are asked about your recognition system, you should be able to point out the details and demonstrate through surveys that the employees appreciate the process and that it contributes to improved employee satisfaction, loyalty, and engagement.

Assessment of workforce engagement, retention, absenteeism, and grievances

We have already discussed this topic in other chapters. The important takeaway for management is to have detailed records that show high levels of performance in each of the workforce factors: engagement, retention, absenteeism, and grievances. In addition, to prove that the levels are high, which can be interpreted as only relative values, we need comparisons to prior surveys, and comparisons to others in the field, industry averages (or standards), or world-class competition. In addition, it helps to show improving trends in these important metrics. And lastly, if these metrics are getting better, it makes those conclusions more credible if you can show what you did to drive the improvement. That way it is not assumed that the metrics improved through a general increase in employee mood based on improving business conditions and perhaps increased participation in the bonus plan, but rather a planned activity intended to improve these factors.

Using a consistent survey instrument to poll employees about their level of satisfaction is a must. It is important to protect against the criticism that surveys tend to measure only what has happened in the last few weeks prior to employees taking the survey. While the halo and horns effects are real, employees should be encouraged to respond with their opinions about the entire year and reserve specific comments for the write-in sections of the survey. Since the workplace is an incredibly dynamic place, you would never conduct any surveys if you waited for a year when there were no unusual events that impacted employee opinions. Since there is always something happening, year-over-year results should be consistent.

Relate engagement to key business results

It is recognized that most businesses are in the business of making money. The corporation generally does things that contribute to profit, and those activities that are not in the interest of improving shareholder wealth are often ignored. Whenever we see a company engaging in community activities, fund-raising, and/or providing special benefits to employees, one of the reasons this is done is to contribute to the bottom line. Happy employees create happy customers (more business). Happy employees work harder because they want to (increase in productivity). When the counting is done, there is usually a payout to the company when they improve employee engagement. It is a true win-win proposition. When audited, a company should be able to translate their employee engagement rates into business results. There should be a relationship between engagement and results. In this way, engagement is a predictor variable for results. Understanding and quantifying this relationship means that the company can impact and control business results by polling and pleasing its employees.

Learning and development systems focus on ethics, performance improvement, core competencies and knowledge transfer from departing employees

Corporate learning and development systems refer to the process of gaining information on the state of each employee's capability, their future needs, and putting in place the resources necessary to develop (introduce) those skills in employees with a customized plan to address each employee's needs. According to the Baldrige Criteria, those areas of particular importance are:

Ethics: There is an increasing demand for ethical behavior on the part of employees, and in particular, managers. Maintaining a continuous stream of information, training, and policy statements between employees and their organizations is a more important element of daily corporate life. Even companies that pride themselves on top ethical standards can be embarrassed by revelations of the actions of a senior manager, as happened to Berkshire Hathaway in 2011.

Performance Improvement: It's not always about working harder. Sometimes we just need to work smarter. When there are technologies available to make our lives more productive and/or eliminate the opportunity for error, are we investing in them? What did we do last year, and how much did we measure its contribution toward improvement in business results?

Core Competencies: Every business has something that they are good at. They have some unique ability others don't have. It becomes their trademark. When we do a SWOT analysis and look at our strengths, weaknesses, opportunities, and threats, the core competencies are our strengths. As much as we need to address our weaknesses by implementing processes to improve these areas, so do we need to capitalize on our strengths. Once recognized as a source of our power over competitors, they will try to neutralize this power by duplicating it or leap-frogging over us. When we have a strength based on our workforce, how can we recognize what it is, and invest our capital to leverage this competitive advantage?

Knowledge Transfer from Departing Employees: We all recognize that the organization invests a lot of time and money into training employees and making them productive contributors on the job. When employees leave they take all that knowledge with them. Those parts of the job that are well documented and can be learned from a procedure manual and standardized training are nothing to be concerned about. However, there are always "those things that we do and know" to make the job better that are lost when an employee leaves. Clearly, an orderly transition where the departing employee can transfer that knowledge to their replacement would be desirable. Is there a process for this to occur? How does the company debrief a departing employee to understand the status of their activities and know what remaining employees can do to keep the ship stable until a replacement can be found? Most employers hold an exit interview with the employee; but coming up with a game plan for the transition seems to be less common.

Career progression

One of the main reasons employees hire into a company is for the promise of career growth. An employer may satisfy this requirement by having a documented process to work with *every* employee to investigate what their desired career progression would be. Just picking out select employees to work with may not be viewed as a systematic process. Employers don't have to worry if there aren't positions available for each employee to be promoted into. Not every employee wants a promotion, nor are all employees worthy of being promoted. The employer simply needs to address the question with each employee in a well-defined process where the needs of both the employee and the employer are discussed to see if further planning and actions are justified. Simply being able to say that many positions are filled from within is insufficient to claim a systematic career progression process.

Walk the Walk

"Go before the people with your example, and be laborious in their affairs." Confucius

Lead by example. A critical factor for superior employee behaviors is to have a superior management team. Employees will not follow a manager whom they believe is unethical or is not a superior performer themselves. Leadership requires that employees want to help the leader accomplish the department's goals because they will follow the leader anywhere. Employees are delighted to work for the leader and learn something by working for and with that leader. This will only happen when the leader is perceived to have unquestionably high character traits.

Advice to Employees (aka, Employees Are Resources)

While trying to help employers hone their skills at building a systematic process to address employee concerns and improve employees' work lives, there is at least an equal need to ground employees in the model that employers have for their workforce.

What defines a good employee? There is no simple answer to that question. Different jobs have different requirements. But here is a good start.

- Arrive on time for your work day. We have heard all the reasons for being late. "I'm not a morning person"; "I watched the football game late last night"; "there was too much traffic this morning"; "I had to stop for coffee and they were brewing a new batch." Nothing succeeds like getting to work on time every day. Make arrangements, leave earlier than you have to in order to overcome the inevitable delays, or make coffee at home, but get to work on time, or preferably a bit early.

- Work diligently all day.

- Depart at the end of the work day without looking at the clock. If it is a few minutes early, it's OK. If it is a few minutes late so you can finish a task that is OK too. If you complete a task and there are at least 10 minutes left in the work day, set up work for tomorrow rather than leaving early.

- If you need to take off early one day to accommodate a personal need, show up early the next day to make up for it. No one should be counting, and you should feel obligated to make up the time.

- Ask for more work when you are not busy. It is impossible for an employer to give you exactly 8 hours of work to do every day. So, when you're not busy, offer to help with another task.

- Don't complain about pay. If your employer thought that the market justified paying you more, and your performance justified paying you more, then you would be paid more. Asking for higher compensation isn't going to result in your employer suddenly saying, "Wow, I'm so glad you brought this travesty to our attention, wait right here while I fill out a pay increase form for you immediately." Employers have compensation policies, salary limits, and salary ranges to follow, which should be adjusted for market conditions each year. They know how much you are worth in the market, or they don't care.

- Don't compare yourself to anyone else, inside or outside the company. You don't know all about that other person's responsibilities or performance.

- Don't ask for anything special. No unusual time off, no excuses, no exceptions. Employers like employees who don't ask for a change in the rules. Please just work within the company's policies and guidelines.

- When you're asked to take on more responsibility for a short time to accommodate a company need, step in willingly. Everyone likes a team player.

- Try to develop a specialty. You will be known for that skill and others will respect you for being their "go-to" person if they have that need.

- Be cooperative. Don't play politics. Don't suck up, and don't stab anyone in the back. Be a team player.

- Keep an eye out for ways to make your job more productive. If you need training, ask for it. If you believe that some software will help you do your job better, propose it.

- Be pleasant. No one gets along with everyone. If you don't like someone, at least treat them with professional courtesy. Working together doesn't always require personal bonding. Accept personality quirks from others just as they accept your personality. If someone offends you, ignore it; and if it persists, seek help from your boss. Try never to offend anyone.

- Do your job to the best of your ability, every day. Make each contribution something you can be proud to call your own.

- Don't argue. There is a time to state your opinion. If your views do not become the prevailing direction, don't pout. Your point has been made and it is on record. Just move on and be a follower/supporter of the current process. The time for one of your ideas to be adopted is just around the corner.

- Be honest and ethical in everything you do. It is easy and tempting to rationalize. Know when you're rationalizing and when you are about to lie.

- Complete things. Having a dozen projects in the works makes you busy, but you have accomplished a task only when it is done and implemented. Don't be in the business of being busy. Move things on to the next stage by completing them.

- Understand and practice good time management. Work very hard to keep your desk clean and ready for the next job to come your way. Then you can address the latest project in real time rather than putting it in the queue and having to prioritize everything all over again.

- Don't ask for anything that others in your position don't have. If your position does not qualify for an office with a door, don't ask for one.

- If someone asks for help, offer it graciously without caring who gets credit for the final result.

- When your employer asks you about your employment satisfaction through surveys, be honest and give them something that they can translate into an actionable plan. When you check off the box that says you rate the cafeteria a 6 out of 10, it is concluding that you don't like the cafeteria. But, what is it that you don't like? Your employer can only change things they understand, so it is much better if you can add a write-in comment and say what it is that you specifically don't like. This becomes an actionable item.

- Be reliable.

This list appears to be sound bites for a "how-to" book. But, taken as a theme, employers want employees to be reliable. The organization is a machine to accomplish a task, and it can do it only as long as the operation of the machine is known and it is working properly. If employees didn't have rules, if they came and went as they pleased, and if the performance of the internal resources weren't reliable, the output of the machine would be of questionable volume, value, and quality. Employees are resources and their performance directly affects the daily output from the business.

I took a tour of a Toyota manufacturing plant some years ago. It was a magnificent facility; clean and well organized. Our tour was about to end around 3 p.m. and there was a plant-wide announcement over the loudspeaker system. It said that the schedule for overtime that day was: Department X: 30 minutes of overtime that day, Department Y: 45 minutes of overtime that day, and Department Z: 45 minutes of overtime that day. They had determined that in order to balance inventory of finished goods, these departments had to work past the normal production hours. For whatever reason, because production had not met standards in some areas, and to get the plant back in balance, it required selected overtime in certain departments on that day.

The same thing happens in an office environment. When someone is not productive, or is out sick, or is not performing to standard for any reason, it throws the process out of balance, even to a small degree. But, these things can escalate to a major problem if not resolved immediately. This isn't to say that there is no flexibility in the schedules in a manufacturing plant or an office environment. But, reliability is a daily requirement, and the more reliable employees are, the better the process will run.

Managers are Different

This list is intended for employees who are generally not management employees. Management employees have different rules for many of these behaviors. For instance, they are expected to work more than 40 hours a week, and as competition in the workforce gets tougher, their need to rise above their peers is often interpreted as working more hours and being desirous of higher visibility. By contrast, non-management employees, whether classified as salaried or hourly, exempt or non-exempt, are the essence of the workforce; and the basic output from the organization is conducted through their efforts. These folks are the "Resources" in Human Resources.

What Came First, The Company or the Employee?

The company existed first, though it couldn't have done much without the employees. The relationship between employees and employers is synergistic. Humble employers give all the credit for business success to their wonderful employees. Employees rave about the work environment their employer has created for them to succeed. Employees are sometimes referred to as "internal customers" to elevate their stature in the organization to those of the customer, or life-blood of the organization. Either way, employers and employees need each other. Anytime one of those entities believes that they hold the upper hand, the other entity shows how much they contribute to the partnership. Employees who say that they "deserve more" or "they'll miss my contribution when I'm gone" are mistaken. No one is irreplaceable.

The company is responsible for creating an environment where you are so pleased to come to work every day that the thought of losing your job is not acceptable to you. If you felt this way you would be so engaged in your job and career that keeping your job would be in the background of your thoughts, and doing a great job would be your main interest. If your company hasn't created that workplace for you, then perhaps you are in the wrong place. Unless a company makes a concerted effort to continuously improve the workplace environment, it isn't likely to change.

If an employee can do better in another department or at another company, they are free to leave. If the relationship isn't working for them, they need to gain happiness elsewhere. It's tough love. Sometimes we hire into a company that isn't a good match for us. Both the employee and the employer made a mistake, and instead of trying to make a square peg fit in a round hole, it is better to part ways. No fault, no harm. The company will survive. In many cases the employee will also survive and may even find an organization that fits better with their needs. Recognize when it's time to implement an exit strategy.

A Wake- Up Call

This is a wake-up call for employees. It isn't all about you, really. If being about you helps the company then it can be about you, but please read the chapter for employers where it says that whenever an employer does something to improve employee engagement, they should be looking for a business benefit directly attributable to that effort. In the same way that doing a good job should translate into salary, benefits, bonus, and other non-cash incentives to you, so will the company look for a return on their investment. As long as you get what you need, you shouldn't care if the company profits from your efforts. It is a mutually beneficial arrangement.

CHAPTER 4: MEASURING EMPLOYEE SATISFACTION

"Employees will only complain or make suggestions three times on the average without a response. After that they conclude that if they don't keep quiet they will be thought to be troublemakers or that management doesn't care." Peter Drucker

The Baldrige Criteria

Whenever we try to formulate a process, it helps to have some framework to use as a standard. In teaching about quality management, I begin by having students think about quality in a holistic way. "If you had a vision that defined a 'good' quality organization, what would that look like?" What characteristics would it have? What attributes could we list that would be demonstrative of high quality? What words would convey the impression of a world-class organization? What would a company have to do if it wanted to be recognized as a leader in quality? What results would the company have to display to provide compelling evidence that it is conducting its business according to the highest quality standards? How would a company compare itself to its competitors and role models in industry to show it is performing at the highest level?

Once I set the stage with those questions, we begin to list those attributes and behaviors that might indicate a company is concentrating on quality initiatives. Most of us have a sense of "quality," but few can get past some individual attributes we believe are indicative of "high quality organizations." The list includes: great products that customers want, best warranty, wonderful customer service, a good place to work, great benefits, open communications, and people-oriented culture; these are among those that we usually list first.

However, when I ask students how they would structure a business around those characteristics, there is that "deadly silence" we all dread in the classroom. In an effort to get the discussion rolling again, and from an overall quality perspective, I usually ask students to start with Deming's 14 Points. It eases them into a framework that defines a quality system from its attributes.

Deming's 14 Points

1. Create and publish a company mission statement and commit to it.
2. Learn the new philosophy.
3. Understand the purpose of inspection.
4. End business practices driven by price alone.
5. Constantly improve the system of production and service.
6. Institute training.
7. Teach and institute leadership.
8. Drive out fear and create trust.
9. Optimize team and individual efforts.
10. Eliminate exhortations for the workforce.
11. Eliminate numerical quotas and M.B.O. Focus on improvement.
12. Remove barriers that rob people of pride of workmanship.
13. Encourage education and self-improvement.
14. Take action to accomplish the transformation.

How many of these basic quality attributes relate to employees? Directly, eight of the 14 points (Points 6 through 13) are focused on the workforce.

Taking the conversation to the next level, I outline the ISO 9000 Certification process and what it provides to structure a business' processes. Then, I bring out the Baldrige Criteria for Performance Excellence and walk through the Categories. Only then can students visualize a structure that a business could create that would contain all those characteristics they listed at the beginning of class. The Criteria touch on the functional areas necessary to achieve high-level performance as a quality organization.

Case Analysis

One of the advantages of having a framework for quality in mind is that it may be used as a standard by which to judge a business case. Once we know what characteristics a company must have to be considered a "quality" organization, we can look at the status of any company and compare it to our "standard." One caveat is that not all characteristics are appropriate to all companies, so being prescriptive in setting our standards has its limitations. However, if we permit a company to omit standards that are not specific to them and the standards are broad enough to be used by a wide variety of business entities, then we may perform a gap analysis on any company.

My students couldn't look at a business case analysis and determine what was good or what needed improvement until they were able to visualize that framework of characteristics, when taken as a system, that represents a company performing at a high level of achievement. The Baldrige Criteria represent the characteristics found in companies that perform at a high level of accomplishment. So, I use it as the framework, or standard, of what a good company looks like.

From the General to the Specific

In the same way, we can use the Baldrige Criteria Category 5 Workforce Focus to structure a high quality, employee-centered organization in our company. If we were to use this same exercise on the business function of workforce focus, we would start by listing those attributes we consider important in making our employees happy. Then we would create a business structure that could contain all those characteristics. What is described next is a process that uses the Baldrige Criteria, and specifically centered on the requirements of Category 5, Workforce Focus. However, no Baldrige Category stands alone in the Criteria. They are all interwoven into a holistic view of an organizational structure intended to result in overall performance excellence. But first, let's see how we would describe a happy employee.

What Makes Employees Happy?

What about pay? Certainly high pay must be the single most important requirement for employees to be happy on the job.

Actually, it is about the fifth reason employees offer as their most important need in the workplace. We can temper that a bit because it depends on the worker. In my experience, there are two segments of the worker population that consider pay to be the most important criterion for them. First is the worker who is paid at a very low rate. The other segment is the employee who defines themselves by their paycheck and has no other loyalty to the job than to provide a service and to be paid.

However, many employees enjoy working and they enjoy the camaraderie of the work environment. To them, happiness is a conglomeration of benefits, empathetic managers, congenial colleagues, satisfying work that is a challenge to them, feeling that they are an important part of the team, feeling that their opinions are valued, growth opportunities in job responsibilities, growth opportunities in lifelong learning, and also, pay. Companies that have loyal employees keep them informed about the workplace environment, ask for suggestions from their employees, and act on those suggestions when it benefits the employees, the company, and the customers.

How Happy are They?

Are your employees happy, satisfied, loyal, or engaged?

Happy: I'm happy: This is a good place to work. I have a job, but not a career. If a better opportunity came along, I would talk. Talk is cheap.

Satisfied: Happy, plus: It would take a lot to get me to leave this place. I'm paid well but not overpaid, the benefits are good, and I work on interesting projects. My boss supports me. I like my boss and coworkers.

Loyal: Satisfied, plus: I've been approached by headhunters and haven't wanted to talk to them. My boss appreciates me. I'm given work that enriches my career, and there is a plan to develop my skills and give me more challenging work that I like. The work environment is friendly and supportive. I enjoy coming to work and believe I have a long-term career ahead of me.

Engaged: Loyal, plus: I actively try to encourage my friends and relatives to work here. When I am away from work, if there is an opportunity, I tell people about my company's products and services to entice them to do business with us. I'm proud to work at my company.

Workforce Engagement

The term "workforce engagement" refers to the extent of workforce commitment, both emotional and intellectual, to accomplishing the work, mission, and vision of the organization. Organizations with high levels of workforce engagement are often characterized by high performing work environments in which people are motivated to do their utmost for the benefit of their customers and for the success of the organization.

In general, members of the workforce feel engaged when they find personal meaning and motivation in their work and when they receive positive interpersonal and workplace support. An engaged workforce benefits from trusting relationships, a safe and cooperative environment, good communication and information flow, empowerment, and performance accountability. Key factors contributing to engagement include training and career development, effective recognition and reward systems, equal opportunity and fair treatment, and family-friendliness.

Engaged employees advocate for their employer because they feel they are valued members of a group. They are not looking to leave, would not easily be convinced to leave, and generally have good attitudes about their job and their work environment. They encourage others to join the company. While the more recognizable term in industry is employee satisfaction, we are moving toward the term loyalty and to a lesser but growing extent, engagement.

Where Does Employee Satisfaction (Engagement) Fit Within the Baldrige Criteria?

There are seven categories within the Baldrige Criteria. They encourage a company to look at six broad business foci to define its business processes. The last category is "Results," which ties together demonstrative metrics to support the claims of successful operations for the six processes in the first categories. One of those work processes is "Workforce Focus."

Focus of the Baldrige Award

The inclusion of "Results" in the Baldrige Criteria is a clear differentiator between a certification, such as ISO 9000, and the Baldrige Award.

ISO 9000 is a series of standards that must be followed in order to display a systematic approach to business operations. At a superficial level, it causes the applicant to document their processes in detail, and then under audit conditions demonstrate that they are doing what they documented. It is a "say what you do, and then do what you said" scenario. It is intended to provide assurance that a company has a consistent approach to its business processes, including processes for analysis and continuous improvement of each segment of operations and also the processes that define the "system". If a company wants to prove to an auditor that they understand their operations, they should define it as a system of inter-related processes. As long as a company complies with the many "shalls" which define the requirements of the standard, they will be certified, or re-certified. However, in contrast to Baldrige, there is no "Results" requirement in ISO certification. Profitability is not a requirement of ISO 9000 certification.

Baldrige, on the other hand differs from ISO 9000 of defining standards for a company to follow, and the Baldrige Criteria permits each applicant to run their business the way that they perceive is best for their market, their industry, and their individual choices. Rather than specifying standards and "shalls," the Criteria asks questions about how the company conducts its business in relation to some factors that have been proven to be effective at world-class companies.

For example, in the Category on Workforce Focus (Category 5), the Criteria asks the following question under 5.1b (2) Workforce Benefits and Policies: How do you support your workforce via services, benefits, and policies? How do you tailor these to the needs of a diverse workforce and different workforce groups and segments? What key benefits do you offer your workforce?

Where Does This Come From?

The Baldrige Criteria are a structured series of suggested descriptors that a company documents to define its management and operational philosophy, processes, and results. To start off, the company that fills out the application must describe its market and regulatory environment, its organizational structure to implement its core strategies and tactics, and its competitive environment, among other details. In this description, the company highlights those attributes it considers important to its success. Two companies in the same industry may perceive different attributes as important to them despite the commonality of their products or services. This may define the uniqueness of each business. The Criteria are not prescriptive in that way. Each of these two companies may have different approaches to the market, to their vendors, or to their employees; and each one may be performing at an extremely high level. It is not the intention of the Baldrige Criteria to dictate the approach a company might take, but rather to see if the company is acting in a way that reinforces its goals and contributes to the success of their chosen approach.

Of course, there are certain deal breakers that reasonable people would argue are not supportive of high-performing organizations. For example, let's say a company required employees, under penalty of termination, to work 20% overtime without compensation, and they stated this as a cost-reducing competitive advantage. Then, reasonable people might consider this to be a flaw in the company's workforce focus regardless of the position the company took that it supported its strategic plan.

Therefore, when an application is evaluated by an Examiner team, they are focused on reviewing the responses of the applicant in light of the attributes the company identifies are important to their success. Filling out the information required by Criteria 7 is a way for the company to demonstrate, with quantifiable results, how successful they have been in organizing an effective plan and implementing the tactics necessary to achieve success.

The Baldrige Criteria Categories

Criteria for Performance Excellence Items and Point Values

Categories and Items		Point Values
1 Leadership		120
1.1 Senior Leadership	70	
1.2 Governance and Societal Responsibilities	50	
2 Strategic Planning		85
2.1 Strategy Development	45	
2.2 Strategy Implementation	40	
3 Customer Focus		85
3.1 Voice of the Customer	40	
3.2 Customer Engagement	45	
4 Measurement, Analysis, and Knowledge Management		90
4.1 Measurement, Analysis, and Improvement of Organizational Performance	45	
4.2 Knowledge Management, Information, and Information Technology	45	
5 Workforce Focus		85
5.1 Workforce Environment	40	
5.2 Workforce Engagement	45	
6 Operations Focus		85
6.1 Work Processes	45	
6.2 Operational Effectiveness	40	
7 Results		450
7.1 Product and Process Results	120	
7.2 Customer-Focused Results	85	
7.3 Workforce-Focused Results	85	
7.4 Leadership and Governance Results	80	
7.5 Financial and Market Results	80	
TOTAL POINTS		1,000

This is one of the defining characteristics of the Baldrige Criteria. Results are weighted as 450 out of 1000 points. In other words, what you do in the organization has to flow through to business success in 5 categories, with workforce focused outcomes as one of those results categories.

Category 5: Workforce Focus

When we ask "What makes employees happy?" there is no shortage of advice we can find from a wide variety of sources. Successful approaches used by companies identified as the "Best Places to Work" are often held up as examples of what to do. However, these approaches may not translate well to many other companies. Therefore, we need to answer that question from the perspective of our employees and not what works well at another company. If we ask them, our employees will tell us what makes them happy. And, in all likelihood, their comments will fall under many of the areas addressed in the Baldrige Category 5 materials. So, let's look at the Category 5 criteria in detail.

The Basic, Overall, and Multiple Requirements of the Criteria

There are three levels of process performance in each category of the Criteria. They are the basic requirements of the category, the overall requirements, and the multiple requirements. As we go further into the details of each sub-process, we find these levels.

If we look at **Category 5**: Workforce Focus, this process category is developed with two Sub-processes. They are:

5.1 Workforce Environment: How do you build an effective and supportive workforce environment? And,

5.2 Workforce Engagement: How do you engage your workforce to achieve organizational and personal success?

Now, let's look at Category 5.2 and its sub-categories:

5.2a Workforce Performance

5.2b Assessment of Workforce Engagement

5.2c Workforce and Leader Development

We further break down category 5.2a into:

5.2a (1) Elements of Engagement: How do you determine the key elements that affect workforce engagement? How do you determine these elements for different workforce groups and segments?

5.2a (2) Organizational Culture: How do you foster an organizational culture that is characterized by open communication, high-performance work, and an engaged workforce? How do you ensure that your organizational culture benefits from the diverse ideas, cultures, and thinking of your workforce?

5.2a (3) Performance Management: How does your workforce performance management system support high performance and workforce engagement? How does it consider workforce compensation, reward, recognition, and incentive practices? How does it reinforce intelligent risk taking to achieve innovation, reinforce a customer and business focus, and reinforce achievement of your action plans?

The Basic Level

The "Basic" level of performance in this example of a process category is the 5.1 and 5.2 level. It is the entry level of workforce focus. A company must be working on building an effective and supportive workforce environment and engaging the workforce for the benefit of the organization and the personal success of the employees to even get in the game.

The Overall Level

The "Overall" level of performance is the a, b, and c level (though some categories only have an a, or an a and b overall level). It is the next rung on the ladder of concentrating on the detailed activities needed to achieve workforce focus. In the 5.2 example, it is: Workforce Performance, Assessment of Workforce Engagement, and Workforce and Leader Development.

The Multiple Requirements Level

The "Multiple" requirements level is the (1)...through... (5) designation, which has a different number of multiple requirements depending on which criteria is being evaluated. In the 5.2a example, it is: Elements of Engagement, Organizational Culture, and Performance Management. As the company responds to each of the multiple requirements in each category, it is encouraged to consider the descriptors given that help give further definition to each of the multiple requirements. No company is expected to have a robust response to every one of the multiple requirements, since some of them might not be critically important to the company's strategic direction. Also, no company is perfect. However, these indicators are considered by the Baldrige organization to be indicative of the kinds of activities common to world-class companies.

How to Interpret Rating Scales

Types of Quantitative Data

There are four types of quantitative data scales. They are:

- Nominal scales
- Ordinal scales
- Interval scales
- Ratio scales

The simplest scale is **the nominal scale**. This scale is used for categorization, such as hot or cold, like or dislike. It conveys a status, but no further information can be gleaned from this data. Nominal data can be used in analysis by proportions; for instance, 76% of respondents have been employed by the company for more than 3 years.

The next scale is **the ordinal scale**, which gives us more information about the data. In an ordinal scale, such as good/better/best, we can categorize the data, but we can also gain information about the order of preference or "acceptability" of attributes. Universities use this scale to categorize students into Freshman, Sophomore, Junior or Senior.

The interval scale is one where differences between ratings are meaningful. This scale is one where we use numbers to substitute for the ordinal scale descriptions. An example would be a question regarding the use of a temperature scale. In this case, the difference between 70 degrees Fahrenheit and 90 degrees Fahrenheit is 20 degrees, and it has the same definition as the 20 degree difference between 120 degrees and 140 degrees. Differences are meaningful, but the value of zero degrees does not mean a total absence of temperature.

The ratio scale incorporates all of the attributes of the nominal, ordinal, and interval scales and adds the feature of an absolute zero. In this way, ratio scaled data can be analyzed using the most sophisticated statistical methods. An example of a ratio scale question would be:

"How many times in the last month did employees arrive to work late?" _____# of times

You can see that 6 times a month is twice 3 times a month and the intervals are also meaningful. Arriving late 8 times as opposed to 6 times is the same increase as being late 4 times in the month as opposed to 2 times. It's not the same percentage increase, but it is the same numerical increase. We can use other mathematical techniques to analyze percentage data. Each of these scales has scaling properties known as:

Assignment for the nominal scale

Order for the ordinal scale

Distance for the interval scale, and

Origin properties for the ratio scale

The next table shows the descriptions for each of these properties. Note that we can use different scales to ask very similar questions. It is how we establish the scales that will determine the analytical methods we must use to evaluate the results of our survey.

Four Scaling Properties: Description and Examples	
Scaling Properties	**Description and Examples**
Assignment property	The employment of unique descriptors to identify an object in a set. **Examples:** The use of numbers (10, 38, 44, 18, 23, etc.); the use of colors (red, blue, green, pink, etc.); yes and no responses to questions that identify objects into mutually exclusive groups.
Order property	Establishes "relative magnitudes" between the descriptors, creating hierarchical rank-order relationships among objects. **Examples:** 1st place is better than a 4th-place finish; a 5-foot person is shorter than a 7-foot person; a regular customer purchases more often than a rare customer.
Distance property	Allows the researcher and respondent to identify, understand, and accurately express absolute (or assumed) differences between objects. **Examples:** Family A with six children living at home, compared to Family B with three children at home, has three more children than Family B; differences in income ranges or age categories.
Origin property	A unique scale descriptor that is designated as being a "true natural zero" or "true state of nothing." **Examples:** Asking a respondent his or her weight or current age; the number of times one shops at a supermarket; or the market share of a specific brand of hand soap.

Choosing Scales

The information we need will determine what scale we will choose. If we want to know how many times our employees contact the HR department, we would not ask a question like: "When you have a problem, do you contact the HR department?" Instead, we would ask: "In the first 6 months after you began your employment, how many times did you contact the

HR department?" The information requirement dictates the question and the scale.

How many options will you offer the employee to focus their response? Let's say you are interested in a continuum of answers from "Definitely Disagree" to "Definitely Agree." Here are several possible choices for scales.

Forced Ranking Scale

Definitely Disagree-Generally Disagree-Slightly Disagree-Slightly Agree-Generally Agree- Definitely Agree

Neutral Scale

Definitely Disagree-Generally Disagree-Slightly Disagree-Neither Agree nor Disagree-Slightly Agree-Generally Agree-Definitely Agree

Ordinal Scale

Definitely Disagree   Definitely Agree

| 1 | 2 | 3 | 4 | 5 | 6 | 7 | 8 | 9 | 1 0 |

Each of these scales differs from each other. In the first scale, we have an even number of potential responses. This is called a forced scale because we are requiring the respondent to take a stand. At the least, they have to choose between slightly agreeing and slightly disagreeing. There is no middle ground.

In the second scale, we are permitting the respondent to choose an answer that is neutral, that they neither agree nor disagree. This is a 7-point scale and allows an "opt out" for those with no preferences or those who don't want to justify their stance. In many cases, when someone uses this answer, it is likely that they have insufficient knowledge of the product or service and use the middle response because they have no opinion, not because their opinion is neutral. It is better to have a response for each question that is "Not Applicable" or "Do Not Know" so those with no knowledge do not skew the data when they are forced to respond with the neutral response.

The third scale is anchored at both ends with a description but permits a more fluid interpretation on the part of the respondent. This can be constructed with 1 through 5, or 1 through 7, or 1 through 10 being the most common numeric divisions.

As you see, we start with the business problem we want to solve, design a research question called a construct that can give us an insight into the cause of the problem, and then choose a scale to measure respondents' answers to the question. Now, what kind of data are we dealing with?

Employee Satisfaction Data

The quantitative data we collect from employee satisfaction surveys is usually a response by the employee answering a question about an attribute that the company provides to its employees. A typical question would be, "Please rate on a scale of 1 to 10, where a rating of 1 means 'Very Dissatisfied' and a rating of 10 means 'Very Satisfied,' your response to the question 'How satisfied are you with our benefit program'?" Of course, this question would be embedded in several questions so that the directions can be given once for all questions that use these scaling criteria.

Looking at the responses and this scale, it is clear that an employee satisfaction scale is an ordinal scale. A rating of 8 is not twice the satisfaction of a rating of 4, and improving satisfaction from 5 to 6 requires a different level of effort than increasing satisfaction from 8 to 9. Since this scale does not have meaningful intervals, nor does it have a ratio property, it is ordinal.

In addition, responses to this scale tend to be skewed to the left, with more people responding on the higher end of the scale than on the lower end. In fact, a typical employee satisfaction histogram looks like the Figure below. This is a survey that I conducted with 123 employees at a construction company a few years ago. It was administered with the "Are We Making Progress" survey used in the Baldrige National Quality Award Program with a survey that, at the time, included the question "I am satisfied." These data are representative of most responses. Note the skewness to the left with most responses in the 4 or 5 categories. It takes a lot for an employee to be so dissatisfied that they rate their employer with a score of 1 or 2.

Ranking Scale	Frequency	Cumulative %
1	2	1.63%
2	6	6.50%
3	11	15.45%
4	63	66.67%
5	41	100.00%
Total Respondents	123	

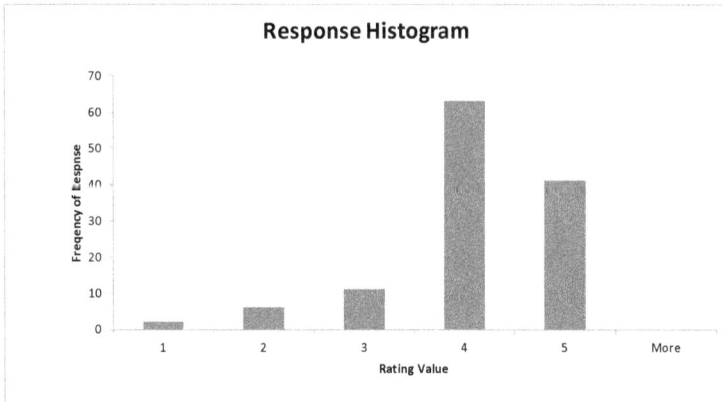

Since this is neither a normal distribution nor does it include data that is more robust than ordinal, it limits the methods that can be used to analyze the employee satisfaction data. At this point, suffice it to say that we need to use methods that are appropriate for ordinal data that does not rely on the assumption of the data falling into a normal distribution.

The next table shows the relationship between scales and the most appropriate measures of central tendency and variation that may be used to summarize the data results, and what the data is telling us.

Relationships between Scale Levels and Measures of Central Tendency and Dispersion				
	Five Basic Levels of Scales			
Measurements Central Tendency	Nominal	Ordinal	Interval	Ratio
Mode	**Appropriate**	Appropriate	Appropriate	Appropriate
Median	*Inappropriate*	**More Appropriate**	Appropriate	Appropriate
Mean	*Inappropriate*	*Inappropriate*	**Most Appropriate**	**Most Appropriate**
Dispersion				
Frequency Distribution	**Appropriate**	Appropriate	Appropriate	Appropriate
Range	*Inappropriate*	**More Appropriate**	Appropriate	Appropriate
Estimated Standard Deviation	*Inappropriate*	*Inappropriate*	**Most Appropriate**	**Most Appropriate**

For those of us who are used to using the mean and standard deviation to understand data, you can see that those are inappropriate measures for ordinal data sets. Rather, median and range are more appropriate to draw statistical conclusions from employee satisfaction surveys.

Let's be clear on this topic. Every distribution has a mean and standard deviation, regardless of the scale appropriate to the data. They are commonly used to look at trends, and this remains a fine way to compare and contrast performance over time and between groups. What we are highlighting is that it is a much better approach to draw statistical conclusions that you want to generalize to the population with statistical tools most appropriate to the scale of your data.

Qualitative Data

There is a certain level of comfort in being able to summarize data in a numerical form. However, we miss out on a lot of rich material when we fail to ask qualitative questions in our surveys. This does not mean having a section for write-in comments after the survey questions are completed. It means that we will seek out answers to qualitative questions that can only be answered by comments, such as:

"Whom do you contact when you have a problem that must be solved immediately?", or

"What could (company) do to increase your level of satisfaction?"

These questions can't be answered with a scale of 1 to 10. These questions are derived from a detailed understanding of your employees' needs. We usually gain this knowledge from talking to our employees. However, there are many avenues to gain this information including:

- Comments in suggestion boxes
- Town Hall meetings
- Manager insights
- Prior surveys
- Focus group discussions

This information is useful in that it gives us the ability to understand the underlying reasons for employee needs. If we show that a metric scored low, we know what to work on. If we asked a question about satisfaction with the cafeteria, and it scored low, say an aggregate rating of 5.3 out of 10, we know that this is a problem, but what causes the problem? The richness of responses to a follow-up question like, "How would you describe the quality of our cafeteria?" will give us many varied responses. We might expect that a respondent would say, "The line is always long and I have to wait a long time to be served. Then, it takes even longer to check-out. And once I sit down to eat, my food is cold!" You can't get that kind of information from a 10-point scale.

Used exclusively, neither qualitative nor quantitative data are enough. It is recommended that every employee satisfaction survey should use a combination of questions specifically designed to accumulate information that is actionable and ready to be implemented to improve satisfaction. There are many advantages of qualitative data, and some disadvantages.

Advantages and Disadvantages of Using Qualitative Research Methods	
Advantages of Qualitative Methods	Disadvantages of Qualitative Methods
•Economical and timely data collection •Richness of the data •Accuracy of recording behaviors •Preliminary insights into building models and scale measurements	•Lack of generalizability •Inability to distinguish small differences •Lack of reliability and validity •Difficulty finding well-trained investigators, interviewers, and observers

Scoring

As we look at the questions that are asked in the criteria for an applicant to demonstrate that they have a good employee focus, we should consider the process we would use to have a robust employee satisfaction score. Let's start with a vision of the result we'd like to achieve, and work backwards.

Within the criteria, we will be scoring the company's activities in several areas and trying to put in place processes that comply with the highest levels of performance. The table below shows how the company would score if their processes are judged in the categories noted. There are four basic areas for consideration:

Approach: Is there a systematic process for employee interaction and concentration on satisfaction?

Deployment: Is the process deployed consistently?

Improvement: Is there a defined process for pursuing improvement in employee satisfaction?

Alignment: Is the process employed in all work groups of the organization?

Note that even a mediocre score of 30% to 45% required fairly high levels of performance, meaning an effective, systematic approach that is mostly deployed. It also represents a company that has initiated an improvement program and alignment of the processes throughout the organization.

PROCESS SCORING GUIDELINES

SCORE	PROCESS (for use with categories 1–6)
0% or 5%	■ No SYSTEMATIC APPROACH to item requirements is evident; information is ANECDOTAL. (A) ■ Little or no DEPLOYMENT of any SYSTEMATIC APPROACH is evident. (D) ■ An improvement orientation is not evident; improvement is achieved through reacting to problems. (L) ■ No organizational ALIGNMENT is evident; individual areas or work units operate independently. (I)
10%, 15%, 20%, or 25%	■ The beginning of a SYSTEMATIC APPROACH to the BASIC REQUIREMENTS of the item is evident. (A) ■ The APPROACH is in the early stages of DEPLOYMENT in most areas or work units, inhibiting progress in achieving the BASIC REQUIREMENTS of the item. (D) ■ Early stages of a transition from reacting to problems to a general improvement orientation are evident. (L) ■ The APPROACH is ALIGNED with other areas or work units largely through joint problem solving. (I)
30%, 35%, 40%, or 45%	■ An EFFECTIVE, SYSTEMATIC APPROACH, responsive to the BASIC REQUIREMENTS of the item, is evident. (A) ■ The APPROACH is DEPLOYED, although some areas or work units are in early stages of DEPLOYMENT. (D) ■ The beginning of a SYSTEMATIC APPROACH to evaluation and improvement of KEY PROCESSES is evident. (L) ■ The APPROACH is in the early stages of ALIGNMENT with your basic organizational needs identified in response to the Organizational Profile and other process items. (I)
50%, 55%, 60%, or 65%	■ An EFFECTIVE, SYSTEMATIC APPROACH, responsive to the OVERALL REQUIREMENTS of the item, is evident. (A) ■ The APPROACH is well DEPLOYED, although DEPLOYMENT may vary in some areas or work units. (D) ■ A fact-based, SYSTEMATIC evaluation and improvement PROCESS and some organizational LEARNING, including INNOVATION, are in place for improving the efficiency and EFFECTIVENESS of KEY PROCESSES. (L) ■ The APPROACH is ALIGNED with your overall organizational needs identified in response to the Organizational Profile and other process items. (I)
70%, 75%, 80%, or 85%	■ An EFFECTIVE, SYSTEMATIC APPROACH, responsive to the MULTIPLE REQUIREMENTS of the item, is evident. (A) ■ The APPROACH is well DEPLOYED, with no significant gaps. (D) ■ Fact-based, SYSTEMATIC evaluation and improvement and organizational LEARNING, including INNOVATION, are KEY management tools; there is clear evidence of refinement as a result of organizational-level ANALYSIS and sharing. (L) ■ The APPROACH is INTEGRATED with your current and future organizational needs identified in response to the Organizational Profile and other process items. (I)
90%, 95%, or 100%	■ An EFFECTIVE, SYSTEMATIC APPROACH, fully responsive to the MULTIPLE REQUIREMENTS of the item, is evident. (A) ■ The APPROACH is fully DEPLOYED without significant weaknesses or gaps in any areas or work units. (D) ■ Fact-based, SYSTEMATIC evaluation and improvement and organizational LEARNING through INNOVATION are KEY organization-wide tools; refinement and INNOVATION, backed by ANALYSIS and sharing, are evident throughout the organization. (L) ■ The APPROACH is well INTEGRATED with your current and future organizational needs identified in response to the Organizational Profile and other process items. (I)

If we want to achieve the highest level score in a Process category, we should have:

- An effective, systematic approach to the detailed items in the criteria
- An approach that is fully deployed throughout the organization
- A fact-based systematic evaluation and improvement in learning, innovation, analysis, and sharing information throughout the organization
- An approach that is well integrated in the planning cycle and consistent with the organization's profile

In order for the company to demonstrate that it has achieved this level of performance, it would have to show that systems are in place to accomplish them, actions have been taken to reach those goals, and that employees confirm, by their opinions, that it has been achieved. Let's remember that each of the questions asked in the Criteria should be addressed through some process that has been documented and implemented throughout the organization. The best way to show this to the Examiner Committee reviewing the applicant's submission is to link the processes in Categories 1 through 6 to results contained in Category 7.

In the "Results" category, we have a different scoring mechanism. We are looking for the level of performance, the trend in performance over time, and comparisons of the company's performance to competitors, best-in-class competitors, and competitors in other industries who provide similar products or services, or who could be used as role models for the industry.

Here are the scoring guidelines for the "Results" category:

RESULTS SCORING GUIDELINES

SCORE	RESULTS (for use with category 7)
0% or 5%	■ There are no organizational PERFORMANCE RESULTS and/or poor RESULTS in areas reported. (Le) ■ TREND data either are not reported or show mainly adverse TRENDS. (T) ■ Comparative information is not reported. (C) ■ RESULTS are not reported for any areas of importance to the accomplishment of your organization's MISSION. (I)
10%, 15%, 20%, or 25%	■ A few organizational PERFORMANCE RESULTS are reported, responsive to the BASIC REQUIREMENTS of the item, and early good PERFORMANCE LEVELS are evident. (Le) ■ Some TREND data are reported, with some adverse TRENDS evident. (T) ■ Little or no comparative information is reported. (C) ■ RESULTS are reported for a few areas of importance to the accomplishment of your organization's MISSION. (I)
30%, 35%, 40%, or 45%	■ Good organizational PERFORMANCE LEVELS are reported, responsive to the BASIC REQUIREMENTS of the item. (Le) ■ Some TREND data are reported, and a majority of the TRENDS presented are beneficial. (T) ■ Early stages of obtaining comparative information are evident. (C) ■ RESULTS are reported for many areas of importance to the accomplishment of your organization's MISSION. (I)
50%, 55%, 60%, or 65%	■ Good organizational PERFORMANCE LEVELS are reported, responsive to the OVERALL REQUIREMENTS of the item. (Le) ■ Beneficial TRENDS are evident in areas of importance to the accomplishment of your organization's MISSION. (T) ■ Some current PERFORMANCE LEVELS have been evaluated against relevant comparisons and/or BENCHMARKS and show areas of good relative PERFORMANCE. (C) ■ Organizational PERFORMANCE RESULTS are reported for most KEY CUSTOMER, market, and PROCESS requirements. (I)
70%, 75%, 80%, or 85%	■ Good to excellent organizational PERFORMANCE LEVELS are reported, responsive to the MULTIPLE REQUIREMENTS of the item. (Le) ■ Beneficial TRENDS have been sustained over time in most areas of importance to the accomplishment of your organization's MISSION. (T) ■ Many to most TRENDS and current PERFORMANCE LEVELS have been evaluated against relevant comparisons and/or BENCHMARKS and show areas of leadership and very good relative PERFORMANCE. (C) ■ Organizational PERFORMANCE RESULTS are reported for most KEY CUSTOMER, market, PROCESS, and ACTION PLAN requirements. (I)
90%, 95%, or 100%	■ Excellent organizational PERFORMANCE LEVELS are reported that are fully responsive to the MULTIPLE REQUIREMENTS of the item. (Le) ■ Beneficial TRENDS have been sustained over time in all areas of importance to the accomplishment of your organization's MISSION. (T) ■ Evidence of industry and BENCHMARK leadership is demonstrated in many areas. (C) ■ Organizational PERFORMANCE RESULTS and PROJECTIONS are reported for most KEY CUSTOMER, market, PROCESS, and ACTION PLAN requirements. (I)

If we want to achieve the highest level score in the results category, we should have:

- Excellent performance levels responding to the detailed items in the requirements
- Beneficial trends sustained over time in all areas of importance to the company

- Evidence of industry and benchmark leadership when compared to competitors
- Performance results and projections for the future, reported for most key customers, market segments, processes, and action plan requirements

So, as we ponder superior employee engagement, we should be thinking about achieving excellence in our processes and in our results according to the Baldrige scoring guidelines.

Now, what do we need to do to get there?

Where Do We Stand Today?

Before we can posit how to get to some future performance goal, we should start with an understanding of where we are today in employee satisfaction, loyalty, and engagement. One way to find out where we are is to poll our employees for their opinions. Luckily, the Baldrige Performance Excellence Program has a survey that may be used to question our employees and managers as to our current condition. If we have never used such an instrument before, we will establish a baseline. If we have a prior history of measuring employee satisfaction but not with this instrument, we also will establish a baseline. If we have used the Baldrige "Are We Making Progress" survey before, then we will use our results to compare with prior surveys to see if we have made progress.

What Do Our Employees Think?

That brings up the question of employees' opinions about the working relationship they have with their employers. One way to employ the Baldrige survey is to send out the questionnaire to each of our employees asking for their opinions. Actually, there are two surveys we can use for polling our employees. One is for use with employees and the other is for use with their managers. I have used both of them. They cover the same attributes, but the form of the question differs from the perspectives of employees and managers. Let's look at the employee survey first. It has 40 questions that ask employees to rate the company's performance in all seven categories of the Baldrige Criteria. It is looking to measure satisfaction with various factors that coalesce into the working relationship employees have with their employer.

ARE WE MAKING PROGRESS?

Your opinion is important to us. There are 40 statements below. For each statement, check the box that best matches how you feel (strongly disagree, disagree, undecided, agree, strongly agree). How you feel will help us decide where we most need to improve or change. We will not be looking at individual responses but will use the information from our whole group to make decisions. It should take you about 10 to 15 minutes to complete this questionnaire.

Senior leaders, please fill in the following information:

_____
Name of organization or unit being discussed
Note: This refers to what is meant each time the word "organization" is used below.

CATEGORY 1: LEADERSHIP	Strongly Disagree	Disagree	Undecided	Agree	Strongly Agree
1a I know my organization's mission (what it is trying to accomplish).	❏	❏	❏	❏	❏
1b I know my organization's vision (where it is trying to go in the future).	❏	❏	❏	❏	❏
1c My senior (top) leaders use our organization's values to guide us.	❏	❏	❏	❏	❏
1d My senior leaders create a work environment that helps me do my job.	❏	❏	❏	❏	❏
1e My organization's leaders share information about the organization.	❏	❏	❏	❏	❏
1f My organization asks what I think.	❏	❏	❏	❏	❏

CATEGORY 2: STRATEGIC PLANNING					
2a As it plans for the future, my organization asks for my ideas.	❏	❏	❏	❏	❏
2b My organization encourages totally new ideas (innovation).	❏	❏	❏	❏	❏
2c I know the parts of my organization's plans that will affect me and my work.	❏	❏	❏	❏	❏
2d I know how to tell if we are making progress on my work group's part of the plan.	❏	❏	❏	❏	❏
2e My organization is flexible and can make changes quickly when needed.	❏	❏	❏	❏	❏

Now, let's compare this to the Managers' survey.

CATEGORY 3: CUSTOMER FOCUS

Note: Your customers are the people who use the products of your work.

	Strongly Disagree	Disagree	Undecided	Agree	Strongly Agree
3a I know who my most important customers are.	❏	❏	❏	❏	❏
3b I regularly ask my customers what they need and want.	❏	❏	❏	❏	❏
3c I ask if my customers are satisfied or dissatisfied with my work.	❏	❏	❏	❏	❏
3d I am allowed to make decisions to solve problems for my customers.	❏	❏	❏	❏	❏
3e I also know who my organization's most important customers are.	❏	❏	❏	❏	❏

CATEGORY 4: MEASUREMENT, ANALYSIS, AND KNOWLEDGE MANAGEMENT

	Strongly Disagree	Disagree	Undecided	Agree	Strongly Agree
4a I know how to measure the quality of my work.	❏	❏	❏	❏	❏
4b I can use this information to make changes that will improve my work.	❏	❏	❏	❏	❏
4c I know how the measures I use in my work fit into the organization's overall measures of improvement.	❏	❏	❏	❏	❏
4d I get all the important information I need to do my work.	❏	❏	❏	❏	❏
4e I know how my organization as a whole is doing.	❏	❏	❏	❏	❏

CATEGORY 5: WORKFORCE FOCUS

	Strongly Disagree	Disagree	Undecided	Agree	Strongly Agree
5a The people I work with cooperate and work as a team.	❏	❏	❏	❏	❏
5b My bosses encourage me to develop my job skills so I can advance in my career.	❏	❏	❏	❏	❏
5c I am recognized for my work.	❏	❏	❏	❏	❏
5d I have a safe workplace.	❏	❏	❏	❏	❏
5e My bosses and my organization care about me.	❏	❏	❏	❏	❏
5f I am committed to my organization's success.	❏	❏	❏	❏	❏

CATEGORY 6: OPERATIONS FOCUS

		Strongly Disagree	Disagree	Undecided	Agree	Strongly Agree
6a	I can get everything I need to do my job.	❏	❏	❏	❏	❏
6b	We have good processes for doing our work.	❏	❏	❏	❏	❏
6c	I have control over my work processes.	❏	❏	❏	❏	❏
6d	We are prepared to handle an emergency.	❏	❏	❏	❏	❏

CATEGORY 7: RESULTS

7a	My work products meet all requirements.	❏	❏	❏	❏	❏
7b	My customers are satisfied with my work.	❏	❏	❏	❏	❏
7c	I know how well my organization is doing financially.	❏	❏	❏	❏	❏
7d	My organization has the right people and skills to do its work.	❏	❏	❏	❏	❏
7e	My organization removes things that get in the way of progress.	❏	❏	❏	❏	❏
7f	My organization obeys laws and regulations.	❏	❏	❏	❏	❏
7g	My organization practices high standards and ethics.	❏	❏	❏	❏	❏
7h	My organization helps me help my community.	❏	❏	❏	❏	❏
7i	My organization is a good place to work.	❏	❏	❏	❏	❏

Would you like to give more information about any of your responses? Please include the number of the statement (for example, 2a or 7d) you are discussing.

_____
_____
_____
_____
_____
_____
_____
_____
_____
_____
_____
_____

ARE WE MAKING PROGRESS AS LEADERS?

Your perceptions as a leader are important to our organization. There are 40 statements below. For each statement, check the box that best matches how you feel (strongly disagree, disagree, undecided, agree, strongly agree). How you feel will help us decide where we most need to improve or change. We also have the opportunity (using the *Are We Making Progress?* questionnaire) to compare the perceptions of our leadership team with those of our workforce to see if there are differences. We will not be looking at individual responses but will use the information from our whole leadership team to make decisions. It should take you about 10 to 15 minutes to complete this questionnaire.

Senior leaders, please fill in the following information:

_____
Name of organization or unit being discussed
Note: This refers to what is meant each time the word "organization" is used below. In addition, "employees" is used interchangeably with "workforce," which includes all people performing work for the organization.

CATEGORY 1: LEADERSHIP	Strongly Disagree	Disagree	Undecided	Agree	Strongly Agree
1a Our workforce knows our organization's mission (what we are trying to accomplish).	❏	❏	❏	❏	❏
1b Our workforce knows our organization's vision (where it is trying to go in the future).	❏	❏	❏	❏	❏
1c Our leadership team uses our organization's values to guide our organization and employees.	❏	❏	❏	❏	❏
1d Our leadership team creates a work environment that helps our employees do their jobs.	❏	❏	❏	❏	❏
1e Our leadership team shares information about the organization.	❏	❏	❏	❏	❏
1f Our leadership team asks employees what they think.	❏	❏	❏	❏	❏

CATEGORY 2: STRATEGIC PLANNING					
2a As our leadership team plans for the future, we ask our employees for their ideas.	❏	❏	❏	❏	❏
2b Our organization encourages totally new ideas (innovation).	❏	❏	❏	❏	❏
2c Our employees know the parts of our organization's plans that will affect them and their work.	❏	❏	❏	❏	❏
2d Our employees know how to tell if they are making progress on their work group's part of the plan.	❏	❏	❏	❏	❏
2e Our organization is flexible and can make changes quickly when needed.	❏	❏	❏	❏	❏

CATEGORY 3: CUSTOMER FOCUS

Note: Your employees' customers are the people who use the products of their personal work.

		Strongly Disagree	Disagree	Undecided	Agree	Strongly Agree
3a	Our employees know who their most important customers are.	❏	❏	❏	❏	❏
3b	Our employees regularly ask their customers what they need and want.	❏	❏	❏	❏	❏
3c	Our employees ask if their customers are satisfied or dissatisfied with their work.	❏	❏	❏	❏	❏
3d	Our employees are allowed to make decisions to solve problems for their customers.	❏	❏	❏	❏	❏
3e	Our employees also know who our organization's most important customers are.	❏	❏	❏	❏	❏

CATEGORY 4: MEASUREMENT, ANALYSIS, AND KNOWLEDGE MANAGEMENT

4a	Our employees know how to measure the quality of their work.	❏	❏	❏	❏	❏
4b	Our employees use this information to make changes that will improve their work.	❏	❏	❏	❏	❏
4c	Our employees know how the measures they use in their work fit into our organization's overall measures of improvement.	❏	❏	❏	❏	❏
4d	Our employees get all the information they need to do their work.	❏	❏	❏	❏	❏
4e	Our employees know how our organization as a whole is doing.	❏	❏	❏	❏	❏

CATEGORY 5: WORKFORCE FOCUS

5a	Our employees cooperate and work as a team.	❏	❏	❏	❏	❏
5b	Our leadership team encourages and enables our employees to develop their job skills so they can advance in their careers.	❏	❏	❏	❏	❏
5c	Our employees are recognized for their work.	❏	❏	❏	❏	❏
5d	Our organization has a safe workplace.	❏	❏	❏	❏	❏
5e	Our managers and our organization care about our workforce.	❏	❏	❏	❏	❏
5f	Our workforce is committed to our organization's success.	❏	❏	❏	❏	❏

CATEGORY 6: OPERATIONS FOCUS	Strongly Disagree	Disagree	Undecided	Agree	Strongly Agree
6a Our employees can get everything they need to do their jobs.	❏	❏	❏	❏	❏
6b Our organization has good processes for doing its work.	❏	❏	❏	❏	❏
6c Our employees have control over their personal work processes.	❏	❏	❏	❏	❏
6d Our organization is prepared to handle an emergency.	❏	❏	❏	❏	❏

CATEGORY 7: RESULTS					
7a Our employees' work products meet all requirements.	❏	❏	❏	❏	❏
7b Our employees' customers are satisfied with their work.	❏	❏	❏	❏	❏
7c Our workforce knows how well our organization is doing financially.	❏	❏	❏	❏	❏
7d Our organization has the right people and skills to do its work.	❏	❏	❏	❏	❏
7e Our organization removes things that get in the way of progress.	❏	❏	❏	❏	❏
7f Our organization obeys laws and regulations.	❏	❏	❏	❏	❏
7g Our organization practices high standards and ethics.	❏	❏	❏	❏	❏
7h Our organization helps our employees help their community.	❏	❏	❏	❏	❏
7i Our employees believe our organization is a good place to work.	❏	❏	❏	❏	❏

Would you like to give more information about any of your responses? Please include the number of the statement (for example, 2a or 7d) you are discussing.

_____
_____
_____
_____
_____
_____
_____
_____

The only difference between the surveys is the perspective of the questions. In the employee survey, a question for employees is:

"I know my organization's mission (what it is trying to accomplish)."

The equivalent question for the senior managers is:

"Our workforce knows our organization's mission (where it is trying to go in the future)."

One way I look at the answers given by these two groups is in the difference between the answers between employees and their managers, which is indicative of the differences in the level of connectedness of the employees versus the managers. In some cases I have seen the managers' responses much higher than those of employees. In following up with both groups, it was found that the managers were much happier in the organization than the employees. They were closer to the top, more privy to detailed information about the company and how it was performing, and they were compensated at a much higher level than their employees with salary, bonus, and perks. In other cases, managers' responses were lower than the employees, and upon further investigation, I found that managers were very critical of their ability to lead and felt that they could have done a better job.

In the case where employees' opinions rate an attribute higher than their senior leaders, I am less concerned than the case where senior leaders rate an attribute higher than the employees, which indicates to me that the leadership team is somewhat disconnected from the employees. They believe they are doing a better job than the employees would confirm.

In any case, a discrepancy between the employees' and managers' responses for the same question is indicative of a mismatch of expectations between the groups. I always look at those discrepancies as an opportunity to find out the underlying reason for the discrepancy.

You may download both surveys in their entirety from www.nist.gov/baldrige/publications

Where Do We Stand Today? (Revisited)

Clearly, the maturity of a company in its performance will determine the goals it sets for itself. For example, if a company does not have a process to define and implement a program that links employee success with business results, then it is not really helpful to set as a goal the "measurement of retention, absenteeism, grievances, safety, and productivity to assess and improve workforce engagement." It's not that these aren't critically important. But, if a company doesn't have high performance on a basic requirement, then alerting it to improve the multiple requirements will do no good because the basic systems aren't in place to support higher-level performance.

In this case, it would be more instructive for the company to understand and engage a system to give employees the resources to succeed in their jobs that have been identified as relevant to, and correlated with, company success. This is a very basic objective. As the company's processes achieve the basic levels of performance, then it may concentrate on higher levels of accomplishment.

This is a prelude to the discussion of measuring and defining a baseline for employee engagement. Once we know where we stand based on employee feedback, we can plan a strategy to improve.

The Detailed Criteria

With this explanation as a backdrop, we can look at the multiple requirements in **Category 5: Workforce Focus**, to gain a perspective on the detailed activities a company should be considering in order to achieve the highest scores in the process and results evaluations. In addition, we want to show links between the different categories and between the multiple requirements and the questionnaire "Are We Making Progress?" survey.

First, let's look at the detailed criteria for Category 5.

The broad objective of Category 5.1 is the workforce environment. It is not simply the physical facility or the benefits offered that make an employee feel comfortable, it is a concern for the systems and processes that a company puts in place to assure that employees have the resources to conduct business in an efficient way and that the workforce is structured to be effective. The notes associated with this category explain the distinction between capability (the knowledge, skills, and abilities to do the work), and capacity (the staffing levels which may change over time to meet customers' demands).

An important element of all the Criteria categories is that a company should not look at its customers or employees through a lens that sees them in a "one size fits all" solution. A company must look at its employees as a grouping of different individuals and departments where the same benefits, work hours, or even policies may not be appropriate for all workers. In other words, does the company segment employee groups with similar needs and customize a work environment that meets the employee's needs while optimizing their contribution to the company.

5.1 Workforce Environment: How do you build an effective and supportive workforce environment? (40 pts.)

Describe how you manage workforce capability and capacity to accomplish your organization's work? Describe how you maintain a supportive and secure work climate.

> Category 5.1a concentrates on the numbers. It is where the company describes its methods to organize a workforce with the right skills and diversity to support the needs of the company. Terms like capability, capacity, core competencies, performance expectations, and action plans are prevalent in this category. It further asks about the nimbleness of the company to plan for and execute changes in employment levels.

Within your response, include answers to the following questions:

Workforce Capability and Capacity

(1) Capability and Capacity: How do you assess your workforce capability and capacity needs, including the skills, certifications, competencies, and staffing levels you need?

(2) New Workforce Members: How do you recruit, hire, place, and retain new members? How do you ensure that your workforce represents the diverse ideas, cultures, and thinking of your hiring and customer community?

(3) Work Accomplishment: How do you organize and manage your workforce to?

- accomplish your organization's work
- capitalize on your organization's core competencies
- reinforce a customer and business focus
- exceed performance expectations

(4) Workforce Change Management: How do you prepare your workforce for changing capability and capacity needs? How have these needs, including staffing levels, changed over time? How do you manage your workforce, its needs, and your needs to ensure continuity, prevent workforce reductions, and minimize the impact of such reductions, if they become necessary? How do you prepare for and manage periods of workforce growth?

> Category 5.1b solicits a response from the company that summarizes efforts to create a facility and policies that are accommodating to the employees. Some of the "Best Places to Work" companies concentrate on this section heavily. Companies provide break areas for employees to unwind, free coffee, daycare services, free lunches, and a host of benefits designed to make the workplace an engaging place to be with a maximum amount of flexibility. This is the place for the company to describe their process of providing a supportive environment to maximize employee comfort and satisfaction with the result that the employee will appreciate their workplace environment and be able to reduce the inevitable stress that comes from their job, angry customers, or tight deadlines which are necessary to perform in a world-class operation.

b. Workforce Climate

(1) Workplace Environment: How do you address workplace environmental factors to ensure and improve workforce health and security and workplace accessibility? What are your performance measures and improvement goals for each of these workforce factors? For your different workplace environments, what significant differences are there in these factors and their performance measures or targets?

(2) Workforce Benefits and Policies: How do you support your workforce via services, benefits, and policies? How do you tailor these to the needs of a diverse workforce and different workforce groups and segments? What key benefits do you offer your workforce?

Category 5.2 asks how the company puts together the incentives and training to assure employees are loyal and engaged. It also wants to see how the company assesses employee satisfaction and engagement. On the assumption that you can't improve something that you haven't measured, having a method for determining a quantitative metric to describe employee engagement is important. Furthermore, this category recognizes that there has to be some benefit to the company for its investment in employee satisfaction. If the company can demonstrate that they have linked employee performance to their level of engagement, they are showing that they understand the interaction of satisfaction/performance as a system which can be managed to the benefit of the employee as well as the company.

5.2 Workforce Engagement: How do you engage your workforce to achieve organizational and personal success? (45 pts.)

Describe how you develop workforce members, managers, and leaders to achieve high performance, including how you engage them in improvement and innovation.

> Category 5.2a is the section that asks about discovering the things that your employees claim will result in higher satisfaction, loyalty, and engagement as well as the efforts the company puts forth to create the culture and environment to reach those goals. It also links the performance management system to the elements of employee satisfaction. One of the questions we should ask is: *Are our results simply based on luck, or can we trace employee satisfaction to a measured and purposeful program designed to build employee satisfaction, loyalty, and engagement?*

Within your response, include answers to the following questions:

a. Workforce Performance

(1) Elements of engagement: How do you determine the key elements that affect workforce engagement? How do you determine these key elements for different workforce groups and segments?

(2) Organizational Culture: How do you foster an organizational culture that is characterized by open communication, high-performance work, and an engaged workforce? How do you ensure that your organizational culture benefits from the diverse ideas, cultures, and thinking of your workforce?

(3) Performance Management: How does your workforce performance management system support high-performance and workforce engagement? How does it consider workforce compensation, reward, recognition, and incentive practices? How does it reinforce intelligent risk taking to achieve innovation, reinforce a customer and business focus, and reinforce achievement of your action plans?

> Category 5.2b deals with our methods of surveying employees to determine their levels of satisfaction, loyalty, and engagement and their suggestions for improvement. It should be noted that a company may use many methods to acquire this information, both formal and informal. Just "walking around" can be a good method to connect with employees; but somewhere, the information gleaned must be collected and used in a way that captures the information (so it isn't lost). A suggestion box may be used. As long as there is a feedback loop to consolidate all the listening posts into a problem-solving process, then any way the company chooses to collect information will be good.

In addition, this category requires a response that links metrics on workforce engagement to the results section of Category 7.

Assessment of Workforce Engagement

(1) Assessment of engagement: How do you assess workforce engagement? What formal and informal assessment methods and measures do you use to determine workforce engagement, including satisfaction? How do these methods and measures differ across workforce groups and segments? How do you use other indicators, such as workforce retention, absenteeism, grievances, safety, and productivity, to assess and improve workforce engagement?

(2) Correlation with Business results: How do you relate findings from your assessment of workforce engagement to key business results reported in Category 7 to identify opportunities for improvement in both workforce engagement and business results?

Category 5.2c identifies the importance of continuous learning for all employees. Not only does it ask about the specific training and development employees receive to do their jobs better, it also asks for measures of effectiveness directly attributable to the learning system. Many companies have training programs. This category digs more deeply into how well the programs are preparing employees to improve their effectiveness and qualify for promotions. It is another closed-loop process. If a company uses their appraisal system to identify employees who are targeted for promotion, develops training programs to fill-in the gaps in knowledge, experience, and ability to be promoted when the occasion arises, and can then measure how well positions have been filled according to those plans, this will be an indication of an effective training and development program.

Workforce and Leader Development

(1) Learning and Development System: How does your learning and development system support the organization's needs and the personal development of your workforce members, managers, and leaders? How does the system

- Address your organization's core competencies, strategic challenges, and achievement of its short-term and long-term action plans
- support organizational performance improvement and innovation
- support ethics and ethical business practices
- improve customer focus
- ensure the transfer of knowledge from departing or retiring workforce members
- ensure the reinforcement of new knowledge and skills on the job

(2) Effectiveness of Learning and Development: How do you evaluate the effectiveness and efficiency of your learning and development system?

(3) Career Progression: How do you manage effective career progression for your workforce members? How do you carry out effective succession planning for management and leadership positions?

Links between Categories

The Baldrige Criteria should be viewed as an integrated system of quality processes. One part doesn't stand alone, though it's easy to think of the different categories as "boxes to check" in completing the application. An example might help to explain the interaction of the categories.

If we look at "Workforce Capability and Capacity" in Category 5.1a (1) (Workforce Focus), it may also be found in Strategic Planning (2.1b [2]), note N5, and (2.2a [4]). It may also be found in Workforce-Focused Outcomes in Results section 7.3a (1), as well as in the "Are We Making Progress" survey Question 5b.

Why is this important? When a Baldrige Examiner is reviewing an application, they are trying to decide many things about the company. Aside from the levels, trends, and comparisons of performance the company presents, it is important that the applicant should display that there is a designed process put in place that can be credited for any improvement in the company's metrics. For instance, if employee satisfaction is measured each year and it is on an upward trend, is there some routine action that the company has employed to effect this improvement?

Say there is a strategic plan to measure and improve employee satisfaction, and a survey is conducted every year. Shortly after the results are summarized, a committee meets to consolidate these results with information collected in the Suggestion Box and documented minutes from the quarterly Town Hall meetings conducted by the company President. There is a subcommittee that works on the ideas from these data to come up with the employee ideas that are most likely to improve satisfaction, and they hold meetings with the management team to determine action items to implement. Then, the ideas that merit implementation are introduced in the workplace.

The next year, surveys compare satisfaction results to last year, and the Town Hall meetings question the effectiveness of the corporate changes intended to improve employee satisfaction.

If satisfaction is improving as displayed in the "Results" Category of the Criteria, we may show that we have a process intended to accomplish this goal. Absent this process and its documentation, we might conclude that any improvement in employee satisfaction is serendipitous and not related to anything we did.

Improvement in employee satisfaction can be the result of a short-term event that is not likely to recur and is not based on any of the suggestions from employees. For instance, when the company has a good year and incentive bonuses are larger than usual, it may improve employees' moods, but that may not be sustainable. So, satisfaction, all else being equal, will go up and down according to how well the company is doing, but it may not address the underlying needs of employees to enjoy their work on a day-to-day basis.

As closure to this example, most employees know that incentive pay, if there is any, is transitory. This may not have much of an impact on overall employee satisfaction if their other needs are met. However, when they have unresolved issues that are obstacles to satisfaction, they may react to any stimulus, such as compensation.

CHAPTER 5: LEADERSHIP'S RESPONSIBILITY IN ACHIEVING EMPLOYEE SATISFACTION

"If your actions inspire others to dream more, learn more, do more and become more, you are a leader." John Quincy Adams

No discussion of employee satisfaction would be complete without a review of Leadership. Research shows that employees hire into a company for the promise of a challenging job, the opportunity for promotion and career enhancement, and professional satisfaction. However, many employees leave their employer because of "people problems," including the relationship they have with their supervisor.

So, how should managers act in order to eliminate concerns about high employee turnover being based on the way they treat employees? Let's look at this from two dimensions: policy and leadership style.

Policy

Since the leadership team must follow and enforce corporate policy, does the organization have policies that are unpopular with employees? Do the leaders poll employees to determine their need for work/life balance issues? Do the company's policies match employee's personal values? For instance, does the company have flexible work hours to accommodate varying employee needs to care for children or meet preferences for work schedules? Or, does the company have very strict 8 a.m. to 5 p.m. work rules?

Leadership Style

Are the managers trained in, and do they practice, collaborative and supportive management techniques? Do the managers offer employees the responsibility and authority to accomplish the work they have been assigned? Are employees given an environment in which they feel that they are appreciated and rewarded for their contributions? As an example, would employees willingly agree to take on extra work to help their manager because they are committed to the manager's success?

These are questions we must answer to gain a perspective on whether leadership is performing at a high level in support of employee satisfaction, loyalty, and engagement. So, what are the tenets of high performing leadership, from the Boardroom to the front-line managers?

Once again, we can refer to the Baldrige Criteria as a template for the scope of processes that a leadership team might engage to support a high quality environment that embraces employee engagement.

How does the Baldrige process define the system that a company puts in place to support the organization achieving its mission? Let's start with a definition of the Leadership system according to the Baldrige Criteria for Performance Excellence.

Leadership System

The term "leadership system" refers to how leadership is exercised, formally and informally, throughout the organization; it is the basis for and the way key decisions are made, communicated, and carried out. It includes structures and mechanisms for decision making, two-way communication, selection and development of leaders and managers, and reinforcement of values, ethical behavior, directions, and performance expectations.

An effective leadership system respects the capabilities and requirements of workforce members and other stakeholders, and it sets high expectations for performance and performance improvement. It builds loyalties and teamwork based on the organization's vision and values and the pursuit of shared goals. It encourages and supports initiative and appropriate risk taking and avoids chains of command that require long decision paths. An effective leadership system includes mechanisms for the leaders to conduct self-examination, receive feedback, and improve.

As in other chapters in this book, we will turn to the Baldrige Criteria to see what attributes a benchmark leadership system might include. It is the leaders of the organization who set the tone of the workplace and, therefore, the environment in which workers must exist. Let's see this in the light of policy.

Consider that a company has a policy that says workers must punch a time clock at 8 a.m. when they start work or face performance and financial consequences, again clock out and in for lunch, and again clock out at 5 p.m. at the end of the workday. Now, we might think that ending this policy would relinquish management's prerogative to control employee's work hours. After all, absent a policy of strict control, wouldn't employees take a laissez-faire attitude to their work hours, simply wandering in whenever they liked and leaving whenever it suited them?

Perhaps we should consider this question from several dimensions.

Job Design

If we design a person's job to be done in 25 hours a week, but they have a 40-hour week obligation, then we have failed to adequately provide enough work for our employee to keep them gainfully employed. So, when they come in late and leave early but still get their work done on time and with high quality, we have no one to blame but management and our job design. We can alternately say that if an employee has to work 50 or 60 hours a week to do their job, we either hired someone who is poorly suited to the work requirements or we are overworking the employee. Since work design is an important factor in employee satisfaction and employer results, we can say that creating an appropriate workload for our employees may eliminate the concern that workers will spend less than 40 hours, on average, on the job. We don't necessarily need time clocks if we engage our employees with meaningful work that takes a standard workday to accomplish.

Management Oversight

Not much is hidden from sight when we work in an organization. Coworkers notice when we come in and when we leave. They notice when we take breaks and when we are making personal phone calls. We are observed by managers who are simply "walking around," which is a common management style.

One of the objections to flexible work hours is that there will be abuse of the work process and some will work less than required. In a system with loose policies, this will be hard to notice. By implementing a strict policy we eliminate abuse, to a greater extent, because everyone will be clocked coming and going, and it is easier to keep track of abuse. On the other hand, most people who care about their jobs understand that they need to work a full day and accomplish their work with high quality standards. So, those employees who fail to follow this rule should be reminded by management. Why punish all workers for the performance issues of a few? Why not have flexibility in work hours and address poor performance when it occurs?

Flexibility for the Workforce without Giving Up Authority

However, there are several versions of "flexible" work hours. In one that is a mix between free reign and specified start and end times, there are "core" hours during which all employees are required to be at work. For instance, all employees must be at work from 9 a.m. to 3 p.m. Then, employees can decide when to arrive in the morning between 7 a.m. and 9 a.m. Once arriving at work, employees are required to work 8 hours (at least). Arrive at 7 a.m. and you can leave by 3 p.m. Arrive by 9 a.m. and you can leave at 5 p.m. and no earlier. It is your choice to flex your time any way you like under this plan.

One advantage of this process to workers is that they get to decide on their workday hours. An advantage for employers is that workers have a hard time getting "personal" time off. If an employee has a 4:00 p.m. dental appointment and they need to leave at 3:30 p.m., then they need to start work by 7:30 a.m. In the past, workers would simply announce they needed to leave early to make a dental appointment and receive "personal" time off. Now, they coordinate their day to deal with the appointment themselves. No approval needed, but no "personal" time off either. (If an employee can't make up the time on the same day, it is ordinarily fine for them to make it up on another day as long as they work at least 40 hours in that week.)

The conclusion we can draw is that it is possible to give up close authority and still retain control over important workplace rules.

Leadership Examples

Characteristics of a Leader

We have all reported to managers who have fine qualities and those who have some undesirable behaviors. Usually, when we assess the leadership style of our executives, we do so through the lens of our personal opinions; in other words, how we want to be managed. Therefore, we can talk to a coworker and say that our manager is fantastic, and then be quite surprised that our coworker thinks just the opposite. How can this same manager be so loved by some and detested by others? The answer is that each of us has a different perspective on what constitutes a good manager. So, we are left to conclude that personal opinions may not be the best method to assess the managerial or leadership skills of our executives.

We need a standard. Such a standard exists in the Baldrige Criteria, Category 1 Leadership. So, let's look at some management profiles and see if we can identify the red flags in these styles that cause us to believe that some improvement can be made. These examples are not based on real people but indicate styles that are meant to get us thinking about areas for improvement. And, since we always learn more from the poor examples than the stellar performers, these companies have somewhat poor managers as illustrations for us. Let's just say that they represent "target-rich environments."

The Inconsistent Power Monger

Ernie is the owner of this privately held company. He inherited the company from his uncle's estate and paid out his aunt for several years. He led a successful business career working for his uncle for 20 years and then owning the company for the last 20 years. Since he has worked in the same business his entire adult life, he believes there is nothing he doesn't know about the organization, and he has personally hired all the employees. Ernie has a sense of entitlement, first by being a big fish in a small pond working for the owner, who was also a relative, and now as a multi-millionaire on his own. He uses the company as his own personal piggy bank, subject of course to the rules of the IRS as he interprets them.

Ernie likes his freedom and holds the purse strings very tightly to keep anyone else from making decisions he doesn't condone. He hates budgets and refuses to set any, or approve any for his direct reports. When asked why he doesn't like budgets as a means of controlling financial actions, he says that budgets are restrictive. He doesn't want anyone to say that they "couldn't go to help a customer because it wasn't in the budget." Most of the employees believe that Ernie doesn't want anyone challenging his frequent trips and entertainment expenses to see if he has overspent *his* budget on the assumption that the Accounting Department would set up a budget for him as well as others and maintain a variance report of his expenditures.

Ernie dislikes formal processes and procedures. He understands the need for documented routine as a means to demonstrate compliance to regulatory standards; however, it is not in his DNA to be restricted from making a snap decision for his favorite people or to display his authority. He might deny a request from one person who wants to ship a product early and then approve it for someone else. No reason or explanation required.

Ernie could be mean when he was in a bad mood. Spreading fear was a favorite pastime for Ernie. He would occasionally walk into an employee's office who was 3 levels below him in the hierarchy and tell the employee that he was unhappy with their performance on a particular job or personally convey a complaint from a customer that was directed at that employee, whether the claim was true or not. It would then take the employee's department manager days to calm them down, get to the underlying cause of the issue, and start on the road to resolving the problem.

Manny, Ernie's son, also worked at the company. Manny was not given much authority and worked for a department manager. There were several times when Ernie was heard to say "I wonder what my idiot son did today?" Manny had a good life despite the difficult environment. While most would have thought that Manny would receive preferential treatment from his father, he did not; he was treated to the same callous outbursts as anyone else in the company. Despite this, Manny was very loyal to the family business and to his father. He was not a comrade of anyone and never took their position when his father had an outburst.

Without formal education or training in management and without having to suffer the threat of being fired, Ernie believed that everyone "really" reported to him, regardless of any "organization chart." He wrote the company's mission and vision statements. He asked for feedback from his managers, but these comments were largely ignored. It was what Ernie wanted that must be achieved and conveyed to everyone inside and outside the company.

Ernie didn't believe in systematic processes to measure customer or employee satisfaction. He believed that "management by walking around" was the best way to assess satisfaction. When Ernie would take his walks around the office and in the shop, he would be available for unsolicited comments from all employees. In some cases when he heard things that troubled him, people would be reprimanded, including the person who "told" Ernie the story. Over time, people would just say "hi" and let him walk on. They knew that anything they told Ernie might come back to haunt them. This did not suit Ernie's needs so he would probe employees for information. Not to appear ungrateful for their jobs, some employees would confess some minor transgression that happened in their department just to keep Ernie happy. Inevitably, a vendetta would then unfold, sometimes for quite trivial issues.

Ernie was completely defined by his company. He literally couldn't distinguish between his personal life and his work life. They simply melded to form his persona. He worked long hours and came and went at his whim. After all, it was his company. He wanted to see people displaying that same kind of dedication by arriving to work early and leaving late (though Ernie never arrived before 9 a.m.) He worked on Saturdays and expected to see his management team there on Saturdays. Employees would rather spend weekend time with their families; however, dedication meant sacrifice to Ernie. When employees did show up on Saturdays he knew that this was simply "face time" and done solely to gain his favorable views of them, but it satisfied him that this was just another display of his power to influence people.

One day the company accountant approached Ernie to tell him that a large customer has just sent in a check in payment for a shipment a second time. It was for a large amount of money (six figures), and he wanted to know what Ernie recommended. (Let's remember that most important and many unimportant decisions were made by Ernie, especially when they represented money transactions.) Ernie said "Hold it aside and don't take it as income. Let's see when they ask for it back. Then, it won't have to be added and subtracted from our income statement." If the company had accounting procedures, any overpayment or double payment would be immediately returned to the customer with an explanation. However, in this context, without any written procedures in accounting, and knowing that Ernie would have an opinion, he was consulted. The customer never discovered the overpayment and the next year, Ernie recognized the income.

Ernie didn't believe in formal performance appraisals. He thought that it was a waste of time to tell someone about their performance when he was doing that every day. No goals needed to be set because goals were too restrictive. If Ernie wanted to change a goal, no document was going to stop him from increasing the sales quota from $9M to $13M, for example, in the middle of the year. He also didn't see any value in asking for employee satisfaction feedback. Employees did what they were told. If they didn't like it, they were in the wrong job. Being told what employees wanted from their jobs was extraneous information to Ernie, and confusing to him. He had a clear understanding of his needs from the workforce and held a dim view of modifying it when the need for modification didn't originate from a new need he had identified. Anyone who complained was disloyal and unworthy of employment.

On many occasions Ernie would walk around in the manufacturing facility. It made him feel that he was close to the workforce. He was very approachable on the shop floor, and the workforce liked that he made himself available to them. But, they were also well aware that anything they said could be used against them. On one of his walks, he was approached by a worker who offered the opinion that there didn't seem to be enough bolts designed into a mechanical structure being manufactured for a customer. The design was a new one and the engineer responsible for the job had done a complete analysis on the project. His design was approved by the engineering manager. However, Ernie took the workers opinion and stormed into the engineering manager's office demanding that more bolts had to be added to the design! That was the opinion of the shop personnel, and he agreed. It certainly appeared to him as well that there were too few bolts. How could this have happened with all the high salaries he paid to engineers? Well, the engineering manager called the design engineer and the company licensed professional engineer into a conference room to review the design. Sure enough, there were enough bolts to carry several times the load required, even with a conservative safety factor. Then the team took their analysis to Ernie. Hearing this confirmation of the design, Ernie went into another tirade and ordered everyone out of his office instructing them to increase the number of bolts immediately.

The Incredibly Consistent Power Monger

Bob had more than his share of luck being in the right place at the right time. He graduated college with a degree in accounting and took a job in his field. Through a series of job changes he ended up at his current employer, a nationwide distribution organization with warehouses in over 100 locations in the U.S. This is a large, publicly held company. Headquarters, where Bob works, is in a Midwest City.

Distributing goods all over the country with consistent results is not an easy task. When you have a universal promise to convey materials within a certain timeframe and with consistent quality in many states, the organization must have repeatable procedures systematically delivered. As an accountant, Bob knows procedures and discipline. He also knows the effects of spending and saving on profitability of the organization.

As Bob became known within the management team, he was respected for his accounting controls and attention to detail. He quickly rose in the accounting function until he was the CFO and reported directly to the CEO. Not long after that, the CEO decided to retire and looked at his management team for a successor. Bob had recently initiated some impressive accounting changes that resulted in a substantial increase in income and earnings per share, and the CEO took notice. He named Bob as the next CEO of the company. With no operating experience, no broad-based managerial exposure, and no understanding of the basic drivers of the industry, Bob was barely 40 years old and the CEO of a publicly traded company.

Although it may be stereotypical in his field, Bob did not have many friends and found it hard to relate to others as equals. As soon as he became CEO, Bob fired all those executive-level managers who had disagreed with him during his tenure. He brought in some functional specialists he had worked with in the past. Now that he had his hand-picked team, he was ready to "roll."

Bob was always "on stage"; and his discussions, even around the water cooler, seemed to be proclamations. Contributions from others were not welcome. In the parlance of some employees, the question asked by all when confronted with a decision was "what would Bob do?" His perceived views were considered in every conversation, and his wrath at not being consulted for the most trivial decision was so painful to bear that no one ever made a decision without asking him first, through the chain of command.

Because of this need for supreme control, he worked long and hard. When he was in the office he arrived by 6:30 a.m. and usually didn't leave until 8 p.m. He was in the office at least one day on each weekend for most of the day. This was probably to justify his enormous salary and bonus, but logistically to find the time to help everyone make all their decisions. All power rested with Bob, and he controlled the organization through incredibly dedicated lieutenants. There was Bob who was the CEO, Chairman of the Board, and President, and a group of Executive VPs, a group of Senior VPs, a group of VPs, and then directors and lower level managers. Any person with a VP title or above was handsomely compensated, which included a generous bonus payout. In years where the operating targets were not met to provide high levels of bonus payout to his officers, Bob would find a way to distribute a "special" bonus to them. They wouldn't do anything to jeopardize their jobs and outsized pay. Anyone who took an independent stand on any issue would find themselves on the street, and this had been proven several times at high and low levels in the organization. Fear of job loss trumped integrity almost every time in this company. If anyone wouldn't do the job exactly as Bob wanted, he would find someone who would.

To Bob, employees were seen as a means to an end. They were not really people, but resources to be exploited. When Bob started at the company, the former CEO created an environment where opinions were respected and basic human needs were accommodated. Within a short time under Bob's tenure, director-level employees could be assigned to an open office space in a noisy cubicle of 10 x 10 feet, a big change from their private offices. Warehouse managers would have to work unscheduled overtime, sometimes 50 – 60 hours a week as salaried employees with no extra pay. The outcome of these changes was high employee turnover, but more importantly to Bob, profit. The Board of Directors and shareholders loved it, and they loved Bob.

One day a warehouse employee sent out an e-mail to all the other warehouses describing a concern he had. It was a heads-up to help them catch the issue before it got out of hand. Bob received a copy of the e-mail and thought that it might leave the company open to criticism. The next day there was a new policy that no one could send out a communication to any group without his approval. No presentations, no e-mail, nothing could be broadcast without the approval of the Department Manager, the VP, the Interstate Shipping Department, the Legal Department, and finally, Bob. Communications came to a grinding halt. Mission accomplished.

Bob relished his position. He had arrived: A young man with a multi-million-dollar-a-year compensation package. He deserved the perks of an expensive company car, private jets, and the corner suite. He distinguished himself from the workforce in several ways outside of compensation. Here's one example. There were two entrances to the building at headquarters. The front door led from a parking lot past the front desk at the center of the building while a side entrance was accessible from a parking lot on the east end of the building. Access was through a key fob. To maintain the exclusivity of the executive staff, Bob had all key fobs programmed to only access the side door except VP level and above. Only the officers of the company had the right (privilege) to enter the building through the front entrance. Even entering and exiting the building indicated status.

Many employees at headquarters wanted to help the outlying warehouses with operations training and general updates. Regardless of the mode of travel or how far the warehouse was from headquarters, no one was permitted to visit a warehouse without the written permission of Bob. His staff was so sensitive to his hatred of headquarters' personnel visiting the warehouses; they simply wouldn't bring him a request for an employee to leave headquarters on a trip. Very few personal training visits ever occurred.

Not a penny could be spent without Bob's signed approval. Headquarters conducted central purchasing for all the warehouse support materials. Shipping skids were purchased on a contract with a single vendor. While skids may be viewed as commodity items which don't change much, there are changes in materials from time to time that create differences in weight and life of a typical skid. If a buyer did an analysis and thought that spending another five cents per skid could result in a better warehouse experience or reduced cost, that buyer had to fill out an approval form and get the signature of their manager, the Department Director, the responsible VP, the Interstate Shipping VP, the Corporate Attorney, and Bob. So averse to spending even a penny more than the current charge, Bob would routinely reject these requests. If a project was important enough to move forward in the view of a Senior VP, they would first approach Bob and get a reading from him about his opinion before bringing the form to him for his review. While this was no guarantee of his approval, it was the way to move anything forward that meant spending money, regardless of amount. No amount was too small to escape Bob's need to exercise final approval.

Let's get back to that skid vendor. As you may imagine, skids are very important in the shipping and distribution field. While there are many competitive skid vendors, Bob had struck a deal with one vendor. This is a company with which Bob maintained a personal friendship with the Senior VP. They apparently knew each other in private life before the opportunity to work together was a possibility. The price deal Bob received was terrific. No one else could touch it. However, because the price was so low, the vendor had a very low margin on the deal. So, when it came to customer service, every time Bob's company needed something, the purchasing agent in charge of skids had a hard time getting the vendor to comply with his request. This made it impossible to keep the warehouses satisfied, and sometimes dysfunctional skids would be used because the vendor was so slow in responding to the complaint. Still, Bob insisted that this vendor should have the exclusive contract. The purchasing agents hated the deal, but Bob wouldn't disappoint his friend, and he wouldn't pay for higher quality.

Is There a Standard for Leadership?

It's easy to say "Wow, what terrible managers!" when reading about these profiles of Ernie and Bob. Their behaviors and values just "feel" wrong. However, without a standard to compare them to, it is a matter of opinion that they are not meeting some absolute framework that defines a good manager or leader.

Another factor to consider when comparing these managers to some standard is the potential benefit of adhering to the standard. In other words, if we act any way we want and get good results, who is to say that we are wrong? What benefit would we achieve if we met some "standard" that we're not attaining by being "ourselves"?

Let's include ego in this equation for a moment. Even if we had some standard and instructed Ernie and Bob in the process and described the benefits to them, neither would likely change. They are not showing that they are students of leadership theory. They are basically bullies, and they will do things their way regardless of the strength of any argument to the contrary. So, when confronted with the question "Are leaders made or born?" my answer is: both. There are those who are simply born with the personality and desire to lead. They come about it naturally. There are some who want to succeed, and while they were not blessed with natural leadership qualities, they are highly motivated to learn. They enjoy the experience and want to be respected as good leaders. They can be taught the skills to lead. Then there are the Ernie and Bob personalities. These are people who rose to executive power through lucky circumstances or excellence in a particular area are their bad behaviors were tolerated because they provided such great organization. Steve Jobs might be in that category. They have the "tricks" of leadership. And they will never be good many courses they take, books they read, or seminars t mean that they can't achieve great business results. ecessarily enjoy working for them.

o see these examples since we should have no prob- believe is "wrong" or in need of improvement with ver, not all management theories would be willing to rs as unacceptable. There was a recent video by a man- who advocated that managers know what to do, and loyees are only there to deliver results based on manage- Anyone who feels the need to disagree with them, offer an r own, or not put in an extraordinary effort to comply with should leave the company or be fired. "Do what I say" is the e not here to think, you are here to carry out my instructions!" ore efficient that way. No time has to be spent debating other inions. "Just get in line, and I'll be much happier."

That's one way to manage. It's on the extreme end of the spectrum, but it is no different than a completely consensus-driven management structure on the other end of the spectrum. In a consensus-driven environment, no decision is final until all members of the team agree on all elements of any decision. As you might expect, many decisions are dead-locked, and no progress can be made.

So, is there a standard for leadership that can be used as a framework to judge whether a manager/leader is following a generally accepted set of principles? Can we show that by following these suggested behaviors we will have better business results than leaders (and their companies) who do not? Is there something that combines the best of both extremes where managers make informed decisions based on employee input and break ties when there is no consensus on an issue? Can managers actually do what managers are supposed to do in decision-making and employees who are closest to the work have substantive input? Let's see if the Baldrige Criteria can help to outline behaviors that can form that framework of cooperative leadership

Here are the specific Criteria related to Leadership.

1 The Leadership category examines how your organi ers' personal actions guide and sustain your organiz your organization's governance system and how your legal, ethical, and societal responsibilities and suppo

1.1   Senior Leadership: How do your senior le

Describe how senior leaders' personal actions guide nization. Describe how senior leaders create an envi engagement, innovation, and high performance. Desc ers communicate with your Workforce and key custome

In your response, include answers to the following questi

a. Vision, Values, and Mission

(1) Vision and Values–How do senior leaders set your organiz and values? How do senior leaders deploy the vision and va your leadership system, to the workforce, to key suppliers an

and to customers and other stakeholders, as appropriate? How do senior leaders' actions reflect a commitment to those values?

(2) Promoting Legal and Ethical Behavior–How do senior leaders' actions demonstrate their commitment to legal and ethical behavior? How do they promote an organizational environment that requires it?

(3) Creating a Sustainable Organization–How do senior leaders create a sustainable organization? How do they

- Create an environment for achievement of your mission, improvement of organizational performance, performance leadership, and organizational and personal learning
- Create a workforce culture that delivers a consistently positive customer expe... ...fosters customer engagement

...r innovative and intelligent risk taking,

...ic objectives, and organizational agility

...ning and the development of future

...al Performance

(. ...aders communicate with and engage
the ...rs? How do they encourage frank,
two-w... ...fective use of social media? How
do they c ...ow do they take an active role in
motivating ...cipation in reward and recognition programs, ...ce and customer and business
focus?

(2) Focus on Action ...reate a focus on action that
will achieve the organiz... ...ve its performance, enable
innovation and intelligent . ...its vision? How do senior
leaders identify needed actio... ...ations for organizational
performance, how do senior lea ...us on creating and bal-
ancing value for customers and o... ...olders?

where... to the... value to the... to learn... no desire to learn... leaders no matter how... That doesn... they attend. That doesn't m... But, employees don't... It is always instructive... lem identifying what w... their behaviors. Howe... discard these behavio... agement consultant... the rest of the emp... ment directives... opinion of the... their directives... mantra; you... It is much... people's o...

1.2   Governance and Societal Responsibilities: How do you govern and fulfill your societal responsibilities? (50 pts.)

Describe your organization's approach to responsible governance and leadership improvement. Describe how you ensure legal and ethical behavior, fulfill your societal responsibilities, and supports your key communities.

In your response, include answers to the following questions:

a. Organizational Governance

(1) Governance System: How does your organization review and achieve the following key aspects of its governance system?

- Accountability for the management's actions
- Fiscal accountability
- Transparency in operations, selection of governance board members, and disclosure policies for those members, as appropriate
- Independence and effectiveness of internal and external audits
- Protection of stakeholder and stockholder interests, as appropriate
- Succession planning for senior leaders

(2) Performance Evaluation: How do you evaluate the performance of your senior leaders, including the chief executive? How do you use these performance evaluations in determining executive compensation? How do you evaluate your governance board members' performance, as appropriate? How do your senior leaders and governance board use these performance evaluations to advance their development and improve both their own effectiveness as leaders and that of your board and leadership system, as appropriate?

Legal and Ethical Behavior

(1) Legal and Regulatory Behavior–How do you address any adverse impacts of your products and operations on society? How do you anticipate public concerns you're your current and future products and operations? How do you prepare for these impacts and concerns proactively, including through conservation of natural resources and effective supply-chain management processes, as appropriate? What are your key

compliance processes, measures, and goals for meeting and surpassing regulatory and legal requirements, as appropriate? What are your key processes, measures, and goals for addressing risks associated with your products and operations?

(2) Ethical Behavior: How do you promote and ensure ethical behavior in all interactions? What are your key processes and measures or indicators for enabling and monitoring ethical behavior in your governance structure, throughout your organization, and in interactions with your workforce, customers, partners, suppliers, and other stakeholders? How do you monitor and respond to breaches of ethical behavior?

Societal Responsibilities and Support of Key Communities

(1) Societal Well-Being–How do you consider societal well-being and benefit as part of your strategy and daily operations? How do you contribute to the well-being of your environmental, social, and economic systems?

(2) Community Support–How do you actively support and strengthen your key communities? What are your key communities? How do you identify them and determine areas for organizational involvement, including areas that leverage your core competencies? How do your senior leaders, in concert with your workforce, contribute to improving these communities?

What Would Ernie and Bob Do?

The question can now be asked. How do we know that Bob or Ernie are managers who need improvement? If we hold them up to the scrutiny of the Baldrige standard, we have a way to judge them within the framework of characteristics that define a high-performing organizational leader.

Baldrige Category	What would Ernie and Bob do?
1.1a(1) Vision and Values	Have some statement, but it will be ignored if it doesn't support their views at the moment.
1.1a(2) Demonstrate a commitment to ethical behavior	Ernie hid the double payment for an invoice.
1.1a(3) Performance improvement, workforce learning, develop and enhance leadership skills, succession planning	This isn't discussed in the profiles. The question is: do these managers appear to be the type to spend money on employee development of any kind?
1.1b(1) Encourage frank 2-way communication, provide reward and recognition for high performance	Both Ernie and Bob tell, they don't ask. Those who disagree with them are fired. High performance is attributable to Ernie and Bob, not their workforce.
1.1b(2) Create/balance value for all stakeholders	This refers to inside stakeholders (employees) as well. There is a lack of concern for a balanced work life toward employees.
1.2a(1) Accountability for management actions	Neither Ernie nor Bob suffer any repercussions for their actions. Ernie owns the company and Bob has a hand-picked Board of Directors, of which he is the Chairman. They are not accountable to anyone for their behaviors.
1.2a(2) Evaluation of senior leaders performance, improvement of personal leadership effectiveness	Ernie is an island. There is no accountability for his actions, and therefore no evaluation of his performance. Bob is evaluated against broad corporate measures established to be easily reached. If he fails to meet them, he can influence the compensation committee to award him a "special" bonus for retention.

1.2b(1) Effective supply chain management	Bob is the skid buyer. If Ernie wanted to insert himself into the buying process, there would be nothing to stop him.
1.2b(2) Promote and ensure ethical behavior	Neither Ernie nor Bob show a concern for ethical behavior in their own actions. However, any one of their employees who violates an ethical standard would be summarily dismissed. This is consistent with the "do as I say, not as I do" philosophy.

Notes:

- This is not to say that all independent business owners are autocratic and mean. They simply have somewhat more control than their publicly traded counterparts.
- Bob has been lucky so far. When employees leave the company they routinely may report to the Human Resources personnel how stultifying the environment is when working with Bob. Everyone in HR knows this, and it is freely admitted. Someday the news will get to the Board, and he will be released from his employment. This can't happen to Ernie.
- The leadership category does indeed consider the impact of leadership actions on employees and their work lives.

Is Employee Satisfaction Important to Business Results

In this context the challenge is to question the benefits of addressing high employee satisfaction when the business is already doing quite well. Are there incremental benefits to the company if they add the value resulting from high performance in employee satisfaction to the other operational performance metrics? Can we do better as a business (results) if employee satisfaction is improved? In other words, should Ernie and Bob change and concentrate on employee satisfaction? What's in it for them? Change isn't easy for Ernie or Bob, so there better be a great payback for going far outside of their comfort zone. And, this takes us back to the argument that happy employees create happy customers. It's a virtuous circle, but it takes a lot of time and effort to accomplish.

This is reminiscent of the argument that investing in quality improvement activities are interpreted by many managers as unnecessary cost. All they see is the upfront cost of training, documentation, organizational changes, hiring a quality manager or team, and living up to the standards of ISO 9000 or Baldrige. They don't see the long-term benefits accruing from quality endeavors. Similarly, investment in employee satisfaction will cost something in the short run and exceed the benefits, but over the long term, improved employee satisfaction leads to increases in customer satisfaction, which should lead to increased sales and higher internal productivity.

One argument goes: Satisfy your employees to the point where they are so happy, that the thought of not having their job would be perceived as a real loss to them. They enjoy coming to work; they work in an enjoyable and supportive environment; and they feel a part of the organization where their needs and wants are addressed. In fact, if they lost their jobs it would be too much of a loss to accept, so they try very hard to be the best employees possible; not just to keep their jobs but because they truly enjoy working for the company.

How to Read the Baldrige Criteria

One way to model "good" leadership is to look at the Baldrige Criteria for Category 1 that we just reviewed. In a way, we can look at the Baldrige criteria as a model for behaviors that will lead a management team to superior performance. What characteristics might be demonstrated by a leader to achieve success in the business as well as offering a useful portfolio of benefits, procedures, and environmental factors aimed at ensuring satisfaction to the company's employees?

Success in business is built on customer satisfaction. Employees are "internal" customers of the organization. Hence, when we satisfy employees, we are addressing the "internal" contingent of our customers. And, we can expect those employees to improve the business' performance as well, because we know that satisfied employees create satisfied customers.

Now that we have reviewed the Baldrige criteria and have linked the criteria language to our two business examples, we are ready to look at the criteria more deeply. What are the different levels of the criteria language? The Baldrige program has evaluated the business results for companies that score highly in the evaluation and for those that don't score highly in the award process. They have conclusive evidence that companies with high scores (mainly winners of the award) meet more of the multiple requirements than companies that don't score as highly, and they enjoy much better business results. This leads us to the conclusion that the more a company concentrates on following the framework of the Baldrige criteria, the more the business will prosper.

The Basic Level

The "Basic" level of performance in this example of a process category is the 1.1 and 1.2 level. It is the entry level of leadership performance. It asks, "How do your senior leaders lead?" and "How do you govern and fulfill your societal responsibilities?"

The Overall Level

The "Overall" level of performance is the a, b, and c level (though some categories only have an a, or an a and b overall level). It is the next rung on the ladder of concentrating on the detailed activities needed to achieve leadership focus.

The Multiple Requirements Level

The "Multiple" requirements level is the (1)…through…(5) designation, which has a different number of multiple requirements depending on which criteria is being evaluated. As the company responds to each of the multiple requirements in each category, it is encouraged to consider the descriptors that help give further definition to each of the multiple requirements. No company is expected to have a robust response to every one of the multiple requirements, since some of them might not be critically important to the company's strategic direction.

Also, no company is perfect. However, these indicators are considered by the Baldrige organization to be indicative of the kinds of activities common to world-class companies. Clearly, if a company isn't performing at the "Basic" level, it is a waste of time to tell them that they are failing at a multiple level requirement. If they have no processes for understanding or measuring "how senior leaders lead," they are much further away from a multiple requirement, such as: create a workforce culture that delivers a consistently positive customer experience and fosters customer engagement. First we work on the basic levels and assure that there is a systematic process underlying leadership. Then we work on the overall level of mission, vision, and values, and then we can get into creating and sustaining the organization.

Results

If we want to achieve the highest level score in the results category, we should have:

- Excellent performance levels responding to the detailed items in the requirements
- Beneficial trends sustained over time in all areas of importance to the company
- Evidence of industry and benchmark leadership when compared to competitors
- Performance results and projections for the future, reported for most key customers, market segments, processes, and action-plan requirements

So, as we ponder superior leadership skills, we should be thinking about achieving excellence in our processes and in our results according to the Baldrige scoring guidelines. Now, what do we need to do to get there?

This is a prelude to the discussion of measuring and defining a baseline for leadership responsibilities. Once we know where we stand, we can plan a strategy to improve.

Leadership Profiles

Do leaders have to be nice? If a leader is successful in running a business, does that mean that they are successful in achieving high performance in each of the criteria within the Baldrige categories? Here is a quote from a review of Steve Jobs, immediately after he resigned his post at Apple. He had been on medical leave and it was obvious that he would not return to the company.

"Steve Jobs is one of the greatest business leaders in American history. This isn't merely a function of Jobs' unimaginable success at Apple since reclaiming the mantle of the company after a forced hiatus, but his entire body of work….[However], for all of his attributes Steve Jobs is also known as one of the most ruthless businessmen and intolerant ball-busters in corporate America today."

This is a quote from a commentary on the Yahoo!Finance site in a segment of "Breakout" on August 25, 2011.

Similar accolades and commentaries have been offered for several other high-profile executives.

So, success in business does not automatically mean that the leaders are nice people and that there is high employee satisfaction. Business success is applauded by stockholders but not necessarily by employees. Success in business sometimes coincides with a very stressful environment where employees are not respected, and this may not necessarily create the environment of a "great place to work." Some employees strive in a competitive environment, and some don't.

Leadership Models

There is no easy way to distinguish between management and leadership. Putting these two essentially different functions into boxes leads us to simplistic definitions. "Managers tell people what to do, and leaders provide the resources for employees to reach higher goals." This is simple but also essentially wrong. It ignores the leader who also has to provide direction and the manager who works cooperatively with employees to set direction and accomplish long-term goals. In most organizations, those in charge must wear both hats to be effective. It is more instructive to think of the percentage of time spent in a leadership role vs. the time spent in the management role. Let's see if we can be clearer about the differences in these two roles.

Prelude

Being a manager is not a bad thing. We often think that the lowest level of workforce coordination is supervision, then we take on more responsibility and become managers, and finally we arrive at a leadership position. The belief is that supervisors are not just low level coordinators; they are unskilled and boorish in their approaches to people. Only when we "grow up" in our roles or gain more education can we become managers. And so it goes to leadership.

In fact, most organizations need supervisors, managers, and leaders to do the daily work of the enterprise. Not only is there a difference in the workforce as we move from shop-floor workers to executive management, there is a difference in the way they communicate. The language of workers is "things" and the language of management is "numbers." The organization requires those who can communicate at the proper levels, and that makes supervisors very important to keep things on track as well as to communicate their needs to the management team. None of our ruminations are intended to diminish the need for or the importance of supervision and management.

Management vs. Leadership

In an article in the Harvard Business Review by Kotter, "What Leaders Really Do," 2001, the difference between management and leadership is summarized. Here is a brief side-by-side comparison.

Management	Leadership
Seek organizational stability	Promote change
Organize people, solve problems, deal with complexity	Prepare the organization for change and provide an environment that supports employees as they cope with change
Planning and budgeting	Sets the direction and articulates the vision for the future
Organizing and staffing, monitors implementation	Achieves the vision by motivating and inspiring

Organize systems that can implement goals and objectives precisely and efficiently	Align all human and other resources to implement the vision and strategies
Provide unambiguous direction	Empower by pushing decision-making down in the organization to its most effective level
Compare system behavior to the plan and make timely adjustments when there is a difference	Motivate employees to ensure that they have the energy to overcome obstacles
Help employees to routinely perform their jobs successfully	Satisfy basic human needs for achievement and self-esteem

When we talk about complexity, it is no small feat to manage a group faced with complex problems. In a recent article by Dr. Harry Hertz, the former Director of the Baldrige Performance Excellence Program, he references a Harvard Business Review article by Sargut and McGrath that defines the transition of business systems from complicated to complex.

The fundamental difference between complicated processes and complex processes is that complicated business systems have many interconnected processes that work in somewhat predictable ways. Given inputs, we may have a detailed model to analyze, but we will usually have a good grasp on the outputs. This is a process that is well handled by managerial talent.

Contrast that to Dr. Hertz's definition of a complex system where the interactions of processes also work in patterned ways, but in the complex environment the interaction of processes may produce different outcomes based on the "sequence and level of interaction."

In these cases, there are more probabilistic outcomes based on very similar inputs. He offers 11 suggestions for "embracing complexity." These suggestions point to a very different management structure for success; it is one that is more inclined toward a leadership style. Here are several of his recommendations:

Recognize your cognitive limitations – "complexity .... is too big for any one individual to address alone."

Seek creative solutions, not complicated structures – "avoid …. adding managerial layers, but create an environment that fosters collaboration."

Reinforce the integrators – "Empower the integrators to lead cultural change through strong role modeling and encouragement by organizational leaders."

Expect rare events – "You must be prepared to expect the unexpected events that require you to respond with agility and adaptability."

Can you imagine Ernie or Bob engaging in these recommendations? Neither of them exhibit leadership qualities and if their businesses grow, it is unlikely that they will have in place a philosophy to deal with the increased business complexity. Their businesses will be stunted, or they will fail because they did not have in-place the necessary methods, and therefore the ability, to respond to rapid change that is required to meet the challenges of customer demands.

Being a Leader Doesn't Mean Abrogating Authority

You have arrived. You're in management. You are in an executive position. Finally! Now I get to make the decisions. You remember the usual process of getting into the ranks of management. Your bosses had done your job, and because they were good at it they were promoted. The bosses made the decisions. You may have suggested some ideas, but the boss decided what would be done. The belief is that once you have arrived in management, you can do all those things you wanted to do, only you were stymied when reporting to those autocratic bosses, because the boss made all the decisions. "When you get to be a boss, you'll be able to make all the decisions. But until then, we'll do it my way!"

The theory behind promoting a good performer to management responsibilities is to leverage their skills on others who could benefit from their ability. For instance, if you were a great design engineer for a fan company, you might now manage a group of five fan engineers and bring your attention to detail, your flair for aesthetics, and your robust mechanical criteria to assist new engineers to learn under your direction. You are supposed to lead and be a mentor.

The flaw in that logic is that there is more to managing than technical skill. And many of those managers who were placed in their positions based on technical competence were ill-prepared to deliver the majority of their responsibilities as managers. Dealing with personnel issues, hiring and firing, performance evaluation, budgeting and cost control, delegation of authority, and goal setting are just some of the new responsibilities placed on the new manager. Usually, they receive no training in any of these skills. And, since we know that managers get work done through others, and this requires "people" skills and not technical skills to a great extent, we may have exactly the wrong person in the job. Couple that with the philosophy that says "when you get to be the boss you can do whatever you want, until then, you'll listen to me," and the cycle continues.

It is a mystery why those bosses don't take a step back and recognize that the organization would have been in much better shape if their old bosses had listened to them years ago. Well, maybe they should act that way and create a cooperative environment in their new management roles.

Pseudo-Leadership

Buzzword Bingo

Some managers create a world of catch phrases and terms to define the direction of their companies. They inculcate this mantra into the thinking and terminology of all employees, and if a memo or presentation doesn't include these buzz words, it is considered lacking in seriousness or attention to the "truly important" mission of the organization. Such terms may be:

Buzzword Bingo			
Customer Delight	ROI Maximization	Empowerment	Human capital
Performance excellence	Stakeholder needs	Process improvement	Optimized performance
Mission	Company vision	World-Class quality	Systems thinking
Don't work harder, work smarter	Top management	The bottom line	Give 110%

These terms are fine when used in an appropriate context. We see them in our literature daily. But it is the preponderance of their usage in a single meeting that makes employees believe that the buzzwords are the essence of the business and not the actions. In one company I know, employees used to bring a sheet with these terms to any management meeting and play "Buzzword Bingo." As employees heard each of the terms they would cross off the square and if they got a line across, a line up and down, or a diagonal line, they would say "BINGO."

Clearly, the importance of the material was discounted, because employees believed that the content was meaningless; it was a play by managers to show how much they were connected with the policies of the company and less on their concerted efforts to actually improve anything. It was a display of managerial loyalty to impress (usually) the President or CEO that their attitudes and lingo are aligned with corporate policy and the criteria that are important to the big boss. These meetings usually end with everyone patting each other on the back for having uncovered and committed to the most important issues, but little will result from the meeting. In my experience, nothing substantive was implemented, but our pseudo-managers sure said all the right things.

Companies with somewhat fewer "insider" terms could make a 3x3 matrix, and truly bad companies could use a full Bingo card with a 5x5 matrix. Elvis said it best when he asked for: "A little less talk and a lot more action."

In fact, a business shouldn't focus on more than one to three "big picture" thoughts. As an example, we might focus on customer satisfaction as our principle driver for our company. Then, all of our plans and actions follow from that direction. We develop our designs, manufacturing process, warranty policy, aftermarket service, pricing, delivery, and hiring philosophy around this one desire: to achieve the highest customer satisfaction we can. Every decision may be measured by asking whether it will enhance customer satisfaction. This would seem to be enough.

Some companies may have other metrics that have special meaning to them, such as those to establish a balanced scorecard, but these are few in number and at a very high level. However, if a company has a matrix of high-level goals that we can enumerate on our "Bingo" card, then they can't possibly pay attention to the details of so many high-level objectives. It has now become a game of displaying your knowledge of buzzwords and not a serious focus on an actionable plan.

Details

Lack of attention to detail is another mark of a pseudo-manager. They ask for superior quality from their employees but fail to perform at a high level themselves. In one case, I was walking through the manufacturing facility with some employees getting a plant tour. I noticed a sign about safety posted throughout the plant. One of my tour guides pointed out that there was a misspelling on the sign. He noted that the message was routinely ignored by employees. When I asked why, he said that employees believed the message was meaningless because if it wasn't important enough for management to get the spelling right, then the message wasn't important either.

This example comes back to the need for leaders to lead by example. If you want excellence from your employees, then make all necessary efforts to point the way with your actions.

Too Much Managerial Distance

Aloofness

One company I worked for had our manufacturing facility right across the hall from my office. As the Engineering Manager, I would routinely (about once a week) walk through the plant with my Quality Manager to keep up to speed on any issues that engineering might be able to solve to improve the quality of our products. These unsolicited walks were in addition to the times I was on the floor helping to facilitate problem solutions for issues that needed immediate attention. After a few months of doing this, I knew all the employees, at least enough to have a conversation with them and understand their job functions, and they knew me.

On one walk, an employee I was talking to asked me to identify the role of a manager who was walking through the shop some distance away. The employee had worked at the facility for 15 years and didn't know the Plant Manager who had worked at the company for over 30 years.

Using the Organization Chart to Isolate Managers

Organization charts convey information about the structure of a company. They show lines of responsibility and reporting relationships. Job titles are usually included. However, in some companies these organization charts are misused. They are used to create barriers to communication. This is referred to as "chain of command." At its worst, employees are forbidden to talk about work with anyone but their direct supervisor, who will take the communication up to higher levels for discussion or approval, if necessary.

Under no circumstance can an employee speak directly to a manager above their immediate boss, thereby skipping the chain of command.

Illusionary Inclusion

Some managers, who don't know how to work cooperatively with employees, have no intention of asking the workers for their opinions (because they believe employees are not in touch with the complexities of the organization), or only trust their own opinions, will employ the illusion of democracy but not the reality of collaborative decision making. These are managers who will ask for opinions after they have already made up their minds. If employees offer views that are in line with the manager's decision, then they have buy-in. If the employees' views differ from the manager's decision, the new input is rejected.

This differs from true collaboration because of the timing of the actual decision making. If the employees' opinions were asked prior to the decision-making process, where they could impact the final decision, it would be great. However, in this case, employees' opinions are asked after the decision was made, making the question disingenuous. In most cases this ploy is well understood by the employees who categorize the manager as autocratic. If this happens repeatedly, employees will be unwilling to offer any suggestions because they see it as a waste of time.

The Stuffed-Shirt

This is a manager who lucked into their job. They have neither the experience nor the scruples to run a business, but somehow they made it. They love the praise heaped on them when their success is held up for review. But, to paraphrase an old expression, "You can tell the true character of a man by what he does in times of adversity."

Think of the leaders of WorldComm or Enron. Think about Bernie Madoff, or those low-level employees at some banks or trading companies who engaged in risky commodities trading racking up huge losses that were hidden with accounting tricks, which finally took down their firms.

It is hard to fathom that any of these "bad" actors came to the table with the intention of defrauding the public. When they rose to power and were successful, it was a drug to them. When hard times hit and they realized that they lacked the skills to succeed on a continuing basis, rather than confess and reach out for talent to help them through, they didn't have the courage and ethical make-up to reveal that they needed help; that they weren't as good as they came to believe. So they lied because they couldn't admit failure.

Even good managers occasionally make bad choices. At the first hint of trouble, a good manager regroups, admits the error, and finds a way to recover. Had those managers simply posted a bad quarter and taken remedial action, they wouldn't be in prison today; billions of dollars wouldn't have been lost to investors because these pseudo-leaders were so full of themselves that they couldn't admit they made a mistake and needed help.

The Mouthpiece

There are managers who are titular rulers. According to Wikipedia this is defined as: "a person in an official position of leadership who possesses few, if any, actual powers." Every organization has them. As such, they make no decisions and may only reflect what the real leader thinks. The only reason they are in their positions is at the pleasure of the real leader who needs a "warm body" to maintain organizational structure.

The true ruler who makes all the decisions is not a leader, but usually a tyrant. You may recognize this as the "Bob" figure in Chapter 5. They trust no one. And, it is well known that no manager can make even simple decisions without asking the tyrant. Managers might even float trial balloons to get a first impression as to the tyrant's leanings on a certain issue before making a proposal for the tyrant to approve. The fear is so great that the tyrant would get so angry at the mere suggestion of an idea, that the manager would get fired on the spot. Many decisions would die with the titular manager because they won't leave themselves vulnerable to suffer the wrath of the tyrant, just for asking him to make a decision that he might not like, thereby tainting their reputation (such that it is). One thing about tyrants is that you can't read their minds, so what might appear innocent to you might make the tyrant really angry. This is considered a bad thing.

So why does the manager stay around when they have no authority? They lack options. They are trapped in their jobs.

Here are two scenarios for our manager under different conditions of the likelihood for them to obtain other employment:

Opportunity to leave is high		
High	Vulnerable	Happy/Loyal
	Gone	Gone
Low		
	Low-----------------High	
	Compensation	

Opportunity to leave is low		
High	Trapped/ Vulnerable	Happy/Loyal
	Gone	Trapped
Low		
	Low-----------------High	
	Compensation	

(Satisfaction — vertical axis, left side of each chart)

So, either the emasculated manager has found other employment or he/she is trapped. Many a tyrant will trap employees into doing their bidding with high pay and the threat of firing if they dare to have an independent thought. This is a strong short-term motivator to keep loyal lieutenants on their staff. The manager becomes a pseudo-leader with the outward appearance of authority but with no ability to lead.

Looking for Trouble

There is a management approach called "management by walking around." The theory is that you can learn a lot about an organization by simply observing. For instance, if you are often visible, you will become a part of the daily activities, as opposed to staying behind a closed door and concentrating on the pile of papers on your desk. While the pile of papers needs to be worked on (or delegated to someone else), you can't understand the company's operations unless you witness the daily activities. Employees become comfortable with your presence if your attitude is to "catch" them "doing something right." You become welcome in their daily lives and you gain a better handle on the details of what makes the company run.

Sometimes you find things that aren't right. This is the fork in the road to determine what kind of leader you are. If your intent is to discover employees doing something right, and there are opportunities for improvement, you can initiate a project to correct the situation by asking the employees to find a way to fix the problem.

On the other hand, you can get mad, berate some employees, and storm off in search of their manager to continue the tirade and demand a solution immediately, or else! In this case, you weren't really looking for employees doing something right, you were looking for trouble. This is the Ernie personality in Chapter 5.

It is easy for employees to quickly decide what kind of manager you are. Do you embrace problems as opportunities for improvement, or do you embarrass employees because problems are intolerable and an insight into their incompetence? Someone has to be punished for this!

I was walking through a company's manufacturing facility with a high-level manager one day. When we crossed the threshold from the offices into the manufacturing plant, I heard an employee whistle. I thought nothing of it; but as we came to a crosswalk, I heard another whistle. The manager who was conducting my tour asked if I had heard the whistle; and I said, yes. He told me that whenever a high-level manager (especially him) walked into the plant, the employees would signal to each other to be on the lookout. It was an announcement that a manager was on the shop floor. They did this by whistling, and the employees could tell where the manager was located in the facility by identifying where the whistles were coming from.

He was proud that he knew their system of announcements and warnings. To him, it was a sign of his stature that employees would recognize his presence and be on their guard. He was important, he could impact their employment, and they knew it. The power of his reputation satisfied this manager. It was not clear to him that this employee behavior was not a positive statement about their feelings for him. Even if he knew this, he didn't care.

It is unlikely that this manager ever learned anything about the workings of the company's operations other than what he saw on an organization chart or performance reports. He was ostracized from the operations knowledge base that could only come from the employees in the shop. His effectiveness was marginalized by what he didn't know. More importantly, this was information that was kept secret from any office employee. He was a report reader/writer and a pseudo manager. When it came to initiating anything meaningful in operations performance improvement, he was powerless not only because he didn't have insight into the needs of the organization, but also because he didn't respect the contributions of operating personnel. He believed that all knowledge worth knowing emanated from management. Employees didn't have anything valuable to share. Asking them questions would be a waste of time.

The Bottom Line

Somewhere, in some Business Schools, some managers were taught that the most important objective for the organization is "a healthy bottom line." This is interpreted as net income. There are many ways to achieve maximum income. Cut costs, drive sales volume, and reduce overhead are three that come to mind. A business is a complicated system with complex interactions between processes. When taken in its strictest sense, the pronouncement that net income maximization should take precedence over all else, the short-term outcome can be really ugly for customers, vendors, and employees.

Some decades ago, a large auto company (let's call it the "company") hired a purchasing executive who had a novel idea. Why not force all suppliers to reduce their prices to the company? The fact that these suppliers had multi-year contracts with the company made no difference to him. Business with the "company" was too important for the suppliers to lose, so he unilaterally tore up their contracts and demanded 20% reductions in their prices across the board. The suppliers were furious. Because these supply contracts were so valuable to any vendor, there already was a lot of competition, and they earned the business by having very competitive prices. Now it was being demanded that they slash 20% off their prices. Many of the suppliers couldn't do it without suffering a loss and had to withdraw.

A company that I was running at the time was a supplier to that auto company. We were lucky. My organization did not make parts for cars or trucks. We manufactured engineered test and production equipment for the company. Here is how it worked:

The auto company would put out a specification and request a quote to at least 5 vendors. They would compile the quotes and pick the lowest bid. They would then take 20% off the lowest bid and put out a proposal to all the original vendors on the list, asking if anyone wanted the business at that price. Since this was highly engineered equipment and very competitively bid, 20% below the lowest bid price would occasionally be around our cost of material for the job. It wouldn't cover the engineering, overhead, or labor, not to mention profit. We had to decline. It would have been a net loss to us to take the order. We could afford to walk away and stay in business, but there were many parts suppliers who went out of business because they lost the work and couldn't survive without sales to that auto supplier. Many employees lost their jobs.

We can only guess what compromises had to be made in overall quality to meet the much lower costs being demanded by the company. It is not possible to make a substantive change in one area, such as cost, and not have it impact on other areas, such as quality. There is an old expression that says, "You can have it fast, you can have it good, you can have it cheap. Pick any two." For that auto maker, one of the choices was cheap. That means there was a compromise in either fast or good, and compromises on either of those choices would be undesirable for the company and the customer. This purchasing executive was a pseudo leader who didn't understand or didn't care about the interactions of the various processes of the company's operations.

These examples are cases where leaders acted in ways that defied good management practice, and the employees and customers suffered.

CHAPTER 6: SETTING EMPLOYEE SATISFACTION GOALS

"Good management is the art of making problems so interesting and their solutions so constructive that everyone wants to get to work and deal with them." Paul Hawken

Three inexorably linked processes for employee satisfaction goal setting are:

- Current satisfaction levels and processes for improvement
- Employee appraisal, and
- Reward systems

If we begin with the ultimate goal of achieving "high" employee satisfaction, we should talk about goal setting first.

Goal Setting

Measuring Satisfaction Levels

If we want to have a meaningful process for satisfaction goal setting, we should first determine the level of satisfaction experienced by our employees. We need a baseline value. That means surveying employees using some means of determining their level of satisfaction with their jobs. There are many ways of doing this, but one method of measuring satisfaction is with the Baldrige "Are We Making Progress" survey. This survey asks for employee feedback based on each of the Baldrige Categories. There are 40 questions in the survey that ask about the working relationship employees have with their employer. By asking questions over a wide range of topics, we can get quite granular in our understanding of specific areas where employees believe that their working conditions may be improved.

Why is it important to measure satisfaction with such detail? It is certainly much easier and less confusing to the employees when they are asked "Are you satisfied with your job?" This approach also makes it much easier to evaluate the results. If we use a 5-point Likert scale, we can use several different approaches to determine satisfaction. For instance:

Response	Percentage of Respondents
Very Dissatisfied	4%
Dissatisfied	12%
Neither Satisfied nor Dissatisfied	23%
Satisfied	44%
Very Satisfied	17%

Or, we could add the top box scores for Satisfied and Very Satisfied and say that 61% of employees are either satisfied or very satisfied. Another conclusion might be that 16% of employees are dissatisfied to some degree.

This is interesting but not actionable data. What makes employees dissatisfied? These results don't give us that information. Of all the potential dissatisfiers in the workplace, what is the major cause of dissatisfaction? If we knew the reason for the vote of dissatisfaction, and making changes to improve satisfaction was consistent with our corporate direction, then we could do something about it.

One method of measuring satisfaction so that we can obtain quantitative data as well as qualitative data is to use the Baldrige "Are We Making Progress" survey. It is aligned to each of the seven Baldrige categories and asks employees to assess their working relationship with their employer.

In the last chapter we reviewed the "Are We Making Progress" surveys. When we use these surveys, it is common to request that employees use the fill-in comments. The comments help us to understand the scores we receive from the survey. As an example, let's take the question "I am allowed to make decisions to solve problems for my customers." From the Category 3 Customer and Market Focus Question 3d, say that we receive a score between "Dissatisfied" and "Neither Satisfied nor Dissatisfied." We now have an assessment of dissatisfaction, but that doesn't tell us what the underlying problem is. Why can't we make decisions? Who or what is standing in the way as an obstacle? Often the fill-in areas will give us that information if we request that employees offer us reasons for the scores they gave.

Once we have information related to why dissatisfaction exists, or satisfaction is low, (let's use these interchangeably, only for the sake of simplicity) we must list the most common reasons for dissatisfaction, decide which ones cause the most dissatisfaction, and finally decide which of the most promising reasons fit with our corporate direction. This decision point may not be intuitive. However, just because employees want something doesn't mean the company must simply say OK! There is that little matter of having a business to run. For example, if employees want to work from home and telecommute, but the business is based on having many scheduled meetings face-to-face with other departments or customers, this may not be a viable option for the company, despite the fact that it would improve employee satisfaction.

Now, we can use typical problem solving methods to brainstorm solutions and come up with recommendations that will implement improvements meant to address issues raised by employees, and specifically aligned to improve employee satisfaction.

Re-measuring Satisfaction Levels

At this point we have determined what actions to take to improve employee satisfaction. We take those actions and then come back at a later date, say in a year, and poll those employees again about the same attributes in the "Are We Making Progress" survey. If we correctly identified the areas that need improvement in the eyes of our employees, and we have implemented the changes, we should note an improvement in employee satisfaction. In addition, those questions that were the basis of our improvement program, for instance, a negative response on Question 3d in the survey, would receive special attention to see if this question demonstrated increased satisfaction. Did we improve employee satisfaction? Did we improve it enough? How much is enough? Did we set a numerical goal?

An Example of This Process

The Malcolm Baldrige National Quality Award process has over 500 volunteers from around the country who act as their Board of Examiners to assess the applications that are received from companies applying for the award each year. These Examiners have credentials as quality experts and have responsible work experience as employees, managers, consultants, and business owners. This means that they may not be representative of the workforce at large.

However, the Baldrige organization polled the Examiner group using their "Are We Making Progress" surveys in 2011. We also have the results from polling of Examiners from 2002/3 and Examiner Leaders from 2004. There are two comparisons that we can make. The first is to compare the opinions of those Baldrige Examiners who were employees in 2011 to Examiners who were leaders in 2011. This is instructive because a mismatch of opinions between company employees and their leaders can be the cause of miscommunication and expectations. As an example, Question 4a in the employee's survey is "I know how to measure the quality of my work," and Question 4a in the leader's survey is "Our employees know how to measure the quality of their work." If we discover that employees rate their ability to measure the quality of their work as 4.6 on a 1.0–5.0 scale, but their leaders think they rate a 3.8 on the same scale, we have a mismatch of opinions. Employees think they are doing a lot better on this attribute than their leaders would say. This becomes an opportunity for improvement. Either employees or their leaders are wrong, or they are looking at the attribute from different viewpoints or requirements. Either way, coming to agreement on this rating will improve communication and expectations.

Here are the results for the 2011 survey comparing employee opinions in each of the seven Baldrige categories with the opinions of leaders.

In these charts, the scoring was made numerical by translating responses to the attributes in the questionnaire in the following way:

Numerical Score	1	2	3	4	5
Respondent Choice	Strongly Disagree	Disagree	Neither Agree or Disagree	Agree	Strongly Agree

Employee Satisfaction 2011 Employees vs. Leadership

■ Employees 2011   ▨ Leaders 2011

	1: Leadership	2: Strategic Planning	3: Customer Focus	4: Measurement, Analysis, and Knowledge Management	5: Workforce Focus	6: Operations Focus	7: Results
Employees 2011	3.94	3.45	4.11	3.72	4.08	3.52	3.91
Leaders 2011	3.94	3.42	3.81	3.31	4.00	3.52	3.84

Employees and leaders both agree that strategic planning and a focus on operations are weak at their companies. While this doesn't speak well of Baldrige examiner's opinions of these two performance categories, at least employees and their leaders are in agreement.

The next conclusion we can draw is that when it comes to Measurement, Analysis, and Knowledge Management, employees believe that they score 3.72 on a scale of 1.0 – 5.0, but leaders rate the employees' ability in this category to be 3.31, a difference of 0.41. In fact, this category was the lowest-rated category by leaders of any category, but not by employees.

It is also telling that these professionals rate the relationship they have with their employers as about 4 out of 5, or 80%. This says that employers have a long way to go for their employees to be satisfied with their work environment. Leaders in those companies believe that their employees' satisfaction with their company's performance criteria is even lower.

So, have things improved since the 2002/3 timeframe for employees? Here is that comparison chart.

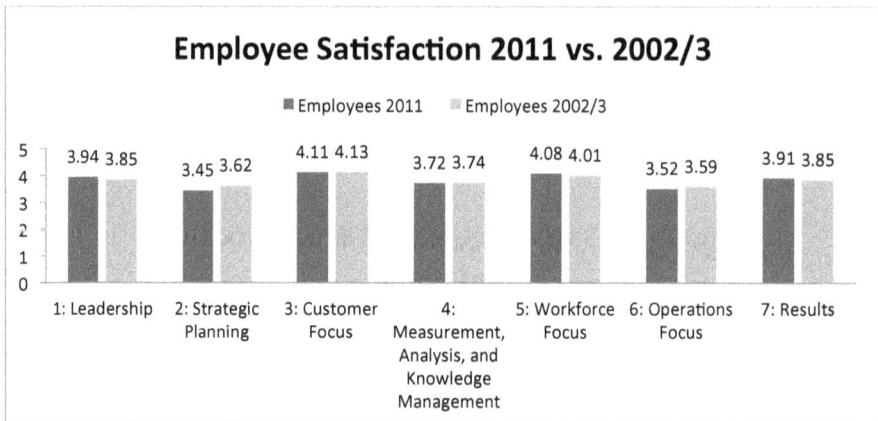

Employee Satisfaction 2011 vs. 2002/3

■ Employees 2011   ▨ Employees 2002/3

Category	2011	2002/3
1: Leadership	3.94	3.85
2: Strategic Planning	3.45	3.62
3: Customer Focus	4.11	4.13
4: Measurement, Analysis, and Knowledge Management	3.72	3.74
5: Workforce Focus	4.08	4.01
6: Operations Focus	3.52	3.59
7: Results	3.91	3.85

Not much progress has been made since the earlier survey of examiners in 2002/3. Despite the fairly negative feedback from the 2002/3 survey, employers haven't made changes that have resulted in an uptick in opinion among their employees. Strategic Planning and Operations focus have been and are still the lowest rated categories in the survey. Remember that a score of 3.0 is the equivalent of a respondent choosing the box "Neither Agree or Disagree." This is a neutral score, and while not a negative, neither is it a positive response.

Once we know our score, how do we establish a reasonable approach to improving our employees' views and how much should we target for that improvement. Is moving an average response of 4.08 in Workforce Focus to 4.15 good enough, or should we target 4.3?

Goal Setting Details

To answer the question about how much is enough improvement in employee satisfaction, we must consider how far away we are from a "reasonable" goal, and what a "reasonable" expectation might be for the resources we are willing to invest in order to raise satisfaction. This brings us to the topic of goal setting. Set the goal too high, and it is a de-motivator because we can't achieve it. Set the goal too low, and it is also a de-motivator; because once you hit the goal, all further effort stops in favor of other goals in other areas that have not been achieved yet.

It doesn't matter where we start, as long as we have an appropriate goal for continuous improvement. The first step is to find out how we are perceived by our employees. Once we decide to measure employee satisfaction, it is not productive to be disappointed in our ratings or the esteem in which we are held by our employees. The purpose of seeking employee feedback is to help us improve, not to punish ourselves over our current relative standing. Seeking feedback and complaints from our employees gives us the ammunition we need to plan our improvement goals.

After all, what would happen if we consistently asked our employees how we could improve and we chose action items directed at improving employee satisfaction each year? We would have a company that truly acted on the advice of our employees and we would enjoy high levels of employee satisfaction. In fact, finding problems should not be viewed negatively. Finding problems means finding opportunities for improvement.

How do we set improvement objectives? One action we must take is to measure the attributes we want to improve. We can't improve something that we can't measure. A second action is to dedicate resources to the project.

Many companies that I work with have difficulty setting improvement goals. Despite my recommendations that a numerical goal is superior to "winging it," they prefer to act on employee suggestions and then "see where we end up at the next survey." If there is improvement, great! If not, we reassess. As long as there is improvement, I encourage my client to continue on their path with the suggestions recommended by employees in the most current survey. If I start to see recurring year-over-year issues that are not being resolved, we have a different conversation.

That begs the question "Would it be better to have set specific goals and see if there is a way to measure improvement toward those goals at intermediate points in the year?" And that asks the deeper question as to the meaning of goals and the motivation that is created by setting goals.

If we set goals too low, we will usually meet them. This may be motivating, but it doesn't result in the best outcome for the company. A certain amount of difficulty should be attendant in reaching goals. Now let's say we set our goals too high and we never reach them. Some managers believe that goals should be set to never be achieved because it will drive employees to always put out more effort in hopes that they will reach these impossible goals. In fact, instead of creating ever greater returns as employees keep pressing for greater gains, this results in a loss of motivation because no matter how hard we work, our need to achieve is never reached, so we stop trying.

For goals to be effective, they need to be based on several criteria:

- Attainable: most of the time
- Specific: a known, measurable outcome that is recognized when achieved
- Mutually agreed upon: by management and the employee or team

Therefore, simply saying "Do the best you can!" is not a clear goal. It is almost impossible to fail in achieving that goal, since no matter where you end up, it can be interpreted as the "best" you can do, all things considered.

Let's consider the goals as represented in the following Figures.

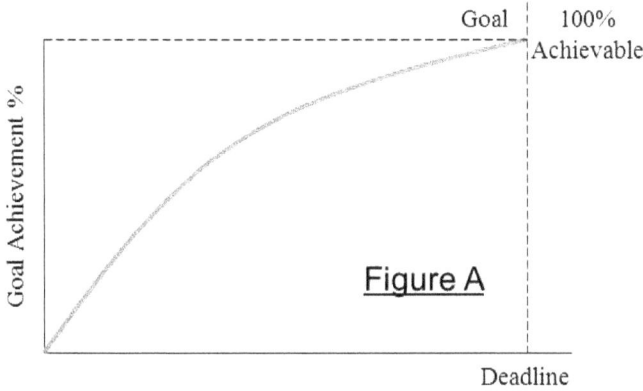

Figure A

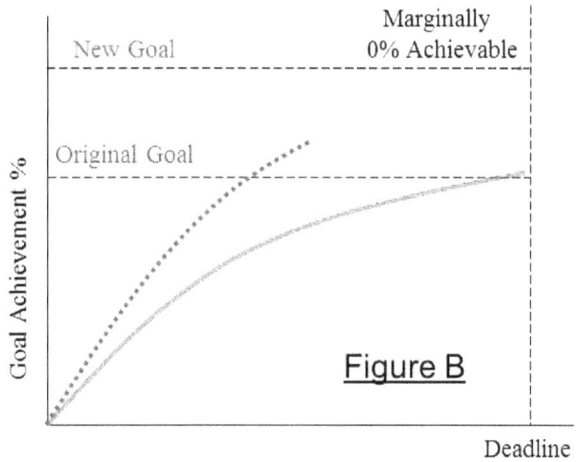

Figure B

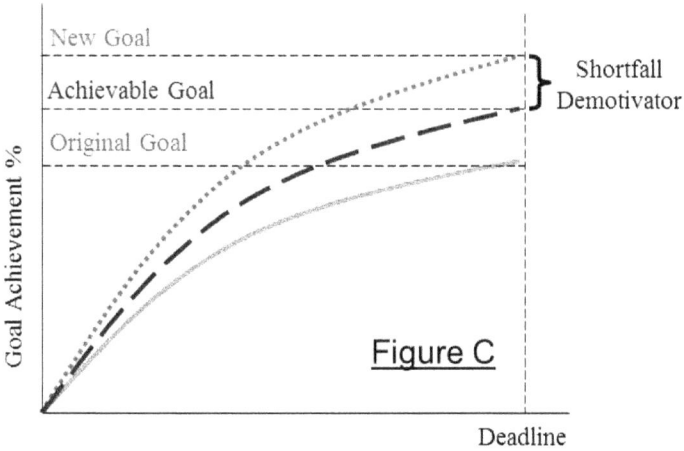

Figure C

In Figure A, we have a low goal and a deadline to achieve it. Research shows that as we approach our goals, we slow down our efforts and there is a diminished marginal return as we get closer to our deadline. We reach the goal very near the deadline. This is caused by the goal no longer being motivational to us. Other goals now become important and we redirect our efforts to other more pressing activities. There is little self-satisfaction in achieving low goals; it is just ticking off another task that has to be achieved. If this low goal is rewarded in a way that is outsized to our perceived effort, then we are confused by the inequity and expect to receive accolades every time we do mundane tasks. This sets the wrong value set to promote superior performance in the future.

Now let's say we overcompensate for this poor goal-setting and instead, set our goals so outrageously high that we never achieve them. This is represented as an overlay in Figure B.

In this case, we never achieve the goal because it is out of reach. When we consistently fail to reach our goals, we stop trying and recognize that success is not to be found in this endeavor, so we move on.

Somewhere between these two extremes, we will have a good goal. Figure C shows this value, but exactly where should we place this goal?

In goal setting parlance, we refer to "stretch" goals, meaning goals that we have to work hard to achieve, but they are within our reach. Those are the most satisfying goals for most employees. In fact, reaching your goals 80% of the time, and coming close the rest of the time, is a good standard to set. It will provide sufficient motivation to succeed, and enough stress to know that without a thoughtful effort you won't get there. And, if we match meaningful rewards to achieving those goals, we can have a very motivating environment to work in.

We use our experience to decide where that goal should be. Sometimes we will be too high and sometimes we will be too low, but that also includes the effects of conditions that are outside of our control. What are some methods that could help us to set meaningful goals?

SMART Goal Setting

To expand on our previous criteria, we could use the SMART method of goal setting. This stands for:

S = Specific

M = Measurable

A = Attainable

R = Realistic

T = Timely

A goal that does not meet the SMART criteria is: "I plan to lose some weight."

A goal that does meet the SMART criteria is: "I plan to lose 5 pounds in the next month."

Specific: Since we can't change or control something that we can't measure, every team should strive to set goals that have a stated outcome, for the simple reason that we need to know when we have achieved the goal. If we lose one pound in the next year, under the first goal of wanting to lose weight we will have achieved the letter of the goal, but not its desired outcome.

Measureable: If the goal can't be measured, then we don't know when we have reached it. If we don't have a scale, how can we tell when we reach our goal of losing 5 pounds, or even measure our progress over time? If we can't discern a successful outcome from failure, we will likely accept poor performance, which we would objectively view as failure.

Attainable: This is the acknowledgment that the goal can be achieved. Once we feel that a goal is unachievable, we stop working on it because our subconscious keeps us from wasting our time.

Realistic: This is closely related to the attainable attribute. However, just because our goals are attainable, that doesn't mean they are realistic. We don't want to set low expectations to achieve realism; we want something that is not only attainable but motivating. We can see progress early, and it moves us to achieve higher performance.

Timely: A goal achieved after the benefits can no longer help the organization is a failure. If we need a new product to be introduced this year to scoop the market, or a cost reduction to be effective this month to protect our profit margins, and they are only realized next year, we have not met our goals, because the temporal factor has not been achieved. It is too late to provide the needed benefits. Telling a child to clean up a room, but giving no time frame, leaves the interpretation of when it has to be done to the child. Telling a child to clean up their room before 6:00 PM tonight gives a definite timeframe for the expectation. That timeframe may be negotiable, but it is not uncertain. The timeframe also must be attainable and realistic to be motivational.

One approach to understanding the scope of the problem is to think about your vision for a perfect result. That becomes the definition of the goal, and everything else is details. Now let's attack the details. What do you need to accomplish in order to achieve the vision of a perfect result? Make a list of all the things you must complete before the vision is realized. It's like making a shopping list for grocery items you must purchase before you can realize that wonderful dinner you envision. It also starts you thinking of the order of actions that must be followed before the end result is achieved. Not only do we have a to-do list, we have a flowchart of the actions necessary to reach our goal.

Setting Objectives

The vision is the first step in goal setting. After that, we want to take those action items and set intermediate objectives. In other words we need to establish the detailed plan to get from where we are to where we envision we want to be. This answers the questions of:

- Who will do each task?
- What role will they play?
- What do we expect of each participant on the team?
- What authority will each team member have?
- What outside resources will we need to obtain?
- Do we need to source training for the team to understand the problem or solution techniques?

- How will we perform periodic reviews of performance?
- What are the measures of success?
- What are the tangible and intangible obstacles to our success? Be honest. Not everyone has the same vision as we do, and some people are willing to, and capable of limiting our success.
- Can our success be a part of the individual performance metrics of each team member?

…..to name a few.

Rewards for Achieving the Goal

Another dimension of goal setting is the assignment of a reward once the goal is reached. For those who diet, it is often said that there should be a reward for reaching the goal. Many believe that a pizza, or ice cream (choose the item you miss most) is a good reward for having lost weight and reached a monthly goal. In fact, there is a theory that a reward of a new pair of pants or a new sweater is a better reward for having achieved a weight-loss goal. So too will we appreciate reaching the goal if we know there is a reward attached to its successful completion. Rewards are most effective if they are given to the team that reached the goal, as well as individuals for their personal contributions to the effort. Rewards should be made public and identified as important to the organization if they are to be most effective.

Where Does Employee Satisfaction Fit in the Organization?

Balanced Scorecard

What are the most important tasks facing the company? Unless there is a stated objective in the mission or values of the company that specifies employee satisfaction/loyalty/engagement, chances are these factors aren't very visible in the organization. However, if a company uses a balanced scorecard to keep their focus on what's important, it is impossible to ignore employee satisfaction when the company optimizes their Key Performance Indicators (KPIs.)

To the outside world of customers and other stakeholders, the balanced score-card is a summary of KPIs in four broad areas. It covers financial metrics, customer perceptions, internal processes, and learning and development. Here is a typical representation of the system:

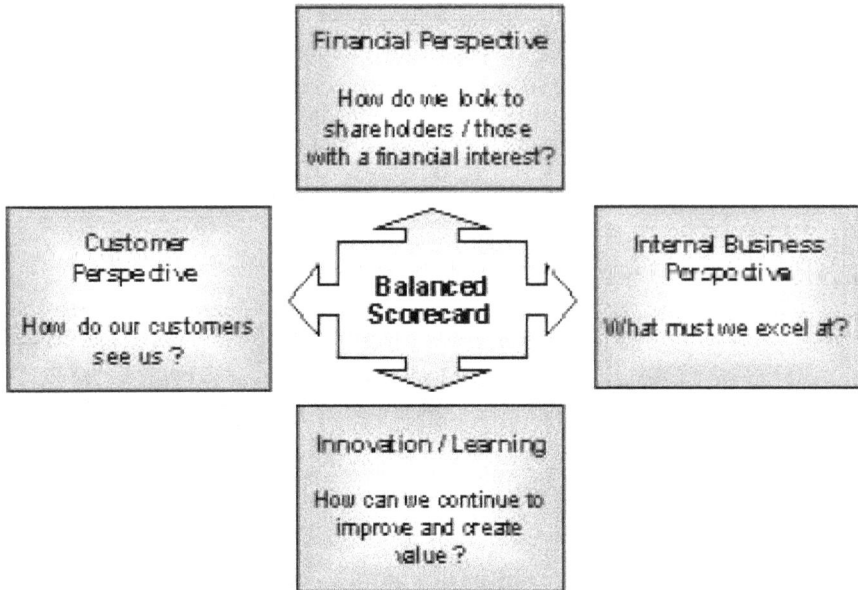

According to "BalancedScorecard.org":

".... financial measures are inadequate .... for guiding and evaluating the journey that information age companies must make to create future value through investment in customers, suppliers, employees, processes, technology, and innovation."

Therefore, we add dimensions to the traditional financial goals and provide a concise report in the areas of highest importance and where we want the most visibility when presenting the results of the organization. It is an aid when presenting to customers and stakeholders so they may gain an understanding of current status, future direction, and improvement since the last report. It is not a replacement for detailed financial statements and strategy or operating statements. Rather, it serves as a high-level summary of our KPIs.

This would appear to be a simple process for concentrating on the "big picture" items that make our business successful. However, to use the balanced scorecard effectively, the idea that summary metrics are built up from more detailed reports must be a part of the system. It is impossible to have a value for innovation and learning without having a method to build the summary based on all those activities we engage in every day. So, as we consider what activities roll up into learning and internal processes, here is a brief outline of some specific performance indicators in an HR Department:

The HR Department would set performance metrics for each of these objectives and roll them up into the overall HR scorecard results. Thus, the build-up of incremental activities in every department creates the summary that we present as our balanced scorecard. And, while it may not be obvious from the four main categories we share with our stakeholders, focus on employee needs is a major part of the business and can be measured in every department in the form of productivity gains, creativity, new product development, cost reduction, or exceeding customer service goals.

Negotiations Between Employers and Employees

We negotiate with our employers in several ways, and it starts when we're looking to be hired into the company. This is perhaps the most obvious negotiation, which encompasses salary, vacation time, and on occasion hiring bonus, moving expense, incentive pay, or working from home, to name a few. Once we're hired, the negotiations usually don't end.

Let's say that we are in our performance appraisal and are told that we need improvement in a certain area. However, the recommendation is based on information that is incorrect, in our mind. Often, it is not a matter of fact that we see our actions and results differently than our manager sees them; it is a matter of perception and interpretation. If we are correct in our interpretation, then we must convince our manager that they are misinformed, or vice versa.

When we are looking to present ourselves for a promotion (and we will assume that this thought has not been on our manager's mind) then we must prepare a case to justify that request.

When we are working to develop our objectives for the next appraisal period, we are trying to find measurable outcomes that are a stretch to reach, but attainable, and that will bring appropriate rewards if achieved. If the rewards are too little, they are not motivational; if they are too large, they send the wrong signal about the value of the accomplishment.

In short, negotiations are all around us in the workplace whether we think of them as "selling" ourselves, correcting a misconception, or iterating toward a rational set of performance objectives. The methods are the same. In fact, the process of negotiation encourages a cooperative relationship to achieve a mutually agreeable outcome, and not an adversarial set of positions where each side gets beat up and the stronger combatant survives with the spoils (and "wins").

A characteristic of the "typical" workplace is that employers think that management prerogative is retained only when managers unilaterally decide who gets promoted, and when; how the "company" sees its employees' performance; or which outcomes are best for the company and should be assigned to its employees. This is the "tell" method of management and stands in stark contrast with the empathetic mode of management. If we believe that decisions are better when we have several minds analyzing the problem, then that should translate into a more cooperative posture when a manager is considering these important career prospects with their employees.

The Process

Whatever we are looking to accomplish in a workplace negotiation, our outlook must be to create value for both ourselves and the organization. There is no reason for the company to provide us with a benefit that doesn't accrue back to the company in some way. Those companies that are counted in the "100 Best Companies to Work For" receive higher customer loyalty and employee satisfaction because of their inclusive policies. Promoting "you" has to be shown to benefit the company in a way that is meaningful to the organization above and beyond how happy you will be with the promotion.

Scope

A negotiation is intended to bring a fair and hopefully amiable conclusion to a deal that provides mutual benefit. Despite the generally optimistic view of this process, it may be conducted under tense conditions with very adversarial partners. Not every negotiation is as easy as "I will cook and you will wash the dishes," or as cooperative as two friends trading baseball cards. Sometimes we are confronted with truly difficult or complex issues such as a divorce with highly charged emotional content. But, whatever the negotiation entails, the process is the same.

Who Leads?

It is often the one who identifies the opportunity who leads. In our business case, it might be the employee who wants a promotion. If the company thought that you were ready for the promotion and there was an opportunity for you to take a more responsible position, they would have approached you. If they haven't approached you with this prospect, but you believe that they are missing a chance to improve the company and your career at the same time, you would feel compelled to bring this to management's attention.

Preparation, Preparation, Preparation

In the realty industry, we hear that the three most important factors in real estate are Location, Location, Location. Well, in negotiation it is Preparation x 3. With that backdrop in mind, the first step in any negotiation is to prepare. The importance of preparation can't be overstated.

I was once in a mock negotiation where I was the head of the union side of a negotiation with management. The theme of this particular workshop was to work on skills for several upcoming contract negotiations. The management teams were placed in this two-day immersive "practice session" where some of us had to assume the side of the bargaining unit for the exercise. One of the lessons coming out of this practice drill was that both sides need to prepare the details of their positions and interests before coming to the table. Here's how it went:

The union side (as expected) had many demands for contract changes. We presented them to management. There was silence. I asked my counterpart on the management team for their list of changes. None were forthcoming. The management team assumed that the negotiation would follow a process of denying any of the union changes or finding some compromise that wouldn't give the union what they wanted, but would give them something. Without anything for management to trade, they lost from the very start. I don't know whether it was laziness on the part of the management team, or that they didn't take the practice seriously, or that they simply believed that their job was to hold changes to a minimum; but that was a terrible loss for the management team. The union ended up with many of their demands, although not at the level first proposed. They still won this negotiation, and management came away with no gain. They got nothing because they didn't ask for anything, and they had not prepared any items to trade against the union's demands. Had management presented some of their own demands, there would have been a much different conversation about trading and offsetting a gain by the union with a gain by management. Each side can get some of what they want, and each side wins. In any negotiation, it is important to prepare with what you want, to be sure, but also what you are willing to trade to get it. That brings us to a method you can use to prepare for a negotiation.

Preparation Checklist

It is not OK to walk into a negotiation with the attitude "let's see what they want, and then we'll come up with a strategy to counter." Before stepping into the room, you should be fully aware of what you want and what you are willing to give up getting it. This is not to say that you can't learn something in the negotiation that might prompt you to change your mind or modify your position or interests. However, if you prepare well enough, you will avoid many surprises that could cause you to have to retreat or revise your strategy.

Here is a brief checklist of those elements you may need in the negotiation:

1. What is the current state of nature? What does the contract look like now? What is the organizational structure today?

2. What are your interests in the negotiation? What is your vision for changes that will meet your needs? Specifically, what would you change and what are the benefits to you? Why do you want these changes, specifically?

3. What are your counterpart's interests? How would they like to change the agreement or the current state of nature? Why do they want these changes, specifically?

4. Where do you start?

5. If you were to make the first offer (which may not be to your benefit), what would it be?

6. If your counterpart were to make the first offer, what do you think it would be?

7. Is there room for an agreeable position somewhere between the two opening offers?

8. If you had detailed information, would you want to make the first offer? If you don't have good information, would it be best to permit your counterpart in the negotiation to make the first offer?

9. What is the absolute minimum you are willing to accept?

10. What is the absolute maximum you are willing to give?

Trade-offs

What would be your bottom line? If you don't get your bottom line you shouldn't accept the deal, so what are you willing to give up in order to achieve the outcome that you feel is absolutely necessary to close the deal?

Back-Up Solution(s)

If you can't get what you want, what is your back-up solution? Do you have more than one back-up solution? For instance, if you don't get the promotion you are negotiating for, do you have another job you can go to that meets your needs? It is much easier to gain a benefit if you have a strong back-up position.

Maintaining the Relationship

Regardless of the outcome of your negotiation it is important to maintain good relationships with your counterpart. No deal has durability if it is not willingly agreed to by both parties, and during negotiation, both parties feel that they have been treated with respect and that their needs were considered important by the other side. How many of us have come to agreement with someone, and the agreement unravels because one side never bought into the final settlement. You may be given the promotion to stop the nagging, but you won't be given the responsibility that goes along with it. You may gain the raise but never get another raise again. These are non-durable agreements and are often the result of not taking into account the feelings of your counterpart in the negotiation.

Interests Differ from Positions

What we really want is our "interest" in the negotiation. What we propose is our negotiating "position." So, when we present our argument, it will be with an offer that is enticing but perhaps not our underlying need. In many cases, requests for promotion mask the real need for an increase in pay. We may not want to take on the responsibilities of a promotion but see it as the only way to make more money or get into a higher bonus pool. It is crucially important to understand the motivations that form our underlying needs and distinguish them from our proposals. This is the difference between our interests and position.

Your Bottom Line

In books on negotiation or conflict management, this is often referred to as the BATNA (best alternative to a negotiated agreement). The BATNA is our best line of defense against accepting an agreement that is bad for us. And, it requires a lot of homework that must be done before the negotiation ever starts.

An example will put the process of determining your BATNA in perspective. Let's say that you are looking to sell your car, and you believe that you can get your best deal by selling it privately. So you plan to put an ad in your local paper to sell the car. You look up the value of your car in the Edmund's guide and it says that a car with your average mileage, in the shape you consider your car to be in, and with the accessories you have in the vehicle, is about $8000. You know that this is an estimate and not a hard price. So you think that you will advertise the car for $8750 and let prospective buyers negotiate with you, and you'll accept $8000, but no less. That is a good strategy. Now you have a buyer who expresses interest in buying your car, but they offered a firm (non-negotiable) $6500 for the car. Should you take the $6500 or not?

Well, we know that $6500 is less than your expected $8000 minimum, but the value of a vehicle isn't an estimate from an online resource or a book; it is what a qualified buyer is willing to pay for it. Now we have a qualified buyer floating a number to us. How do we know if it is the best we can do or even if it's a good number? We need to have a BATNA. In other words, if we decline the offer of $6500, what would we do that is better than the offer on the table? If we have no other place to go, and perhaps we had other offers that were below $6500, should we consider taking this offer? What is our Best Alternative to a Negotiated Agreement?

The Benefit of Having a BATNA

It should be clear now that the only way to assess an offer from your counterpart is to be able to compare it to some other solution. Therefore:

- The better your BATNA the stronger will be your negotiation ability, since you can always decline the deal you are negotiating and go to your BATNA.
- Having a BATNA keeps you from slipping into a bad deal because you know the level at which you can call off the negotiation, rather than being dragged into a bad deal.

The BATNA offers us several other advantages. Even if we don't have an acceptable walk-away option, knowing when to cut off negotiations and continue to search for alternatives is valuable. We have no power in the process if we don't have an acceptable BATNA. Every offer we make is baseless, and it is only by luck that we can bluff our way into a good deal without having an alternative to back it up. Our appearance of strength can be easily challenged by asking us for a justification for our position (which is exactly our tactic when given an unreasonable offer by our counterpart). Having none, our position is uncovered. There is no better argument than to have another offer to claim as our BATNA. In the car negotiation above, if we had an offer from a dealer that they would give us $7800 for our car, the $6500 offer is revealed as insufficient. Without such a BATNA, the $6500 offer can't be parried effectively.

Uncovering Your Counterpart's Interests

There is an old story about two sisters who are arguing about an orange. Each sister wants the orange, and they are in a spirited discussion when their mother walks into the room. Noting the disagreement, mom cuts the orange in two and gives each sister half. We would call that compromise. Neither sister really wins the orange, but both sisters have something in the bargain. The sisters separate and one sister peels her half of the orange and eats the fruit. The peel is discarded. The other sister peels the orange and uses her half of the peel for zest in a cake recipe she is preparing, and she throws away the fruit. What we have just described in this story is this:

> Conflict that is resolved by compromise may not result in the best outcome… and, both sisters expressed their *positions* while arguing, not their *interests*. When confronted by conflict it is often instructive to ask the question "why do you want this?" and discover the underlying benefits accruing to your counterpart by having their position met. It is like the employee who wants a promotion because they believe that is the only way they can make more money, despite the fact that they might hate the job responsibilities of the new job. In our sisters/orange scenario, had they discussed with each other their real underlying interests in the orange, each sister could have had the entire orange for their individual purposes.

This is not such a trumped-up scenario. I was involved in a discussion with a customer a few years ago that sounded like a mismatch of positions to me. The customer wanted to order an expensive piece of equipment from my company and they needed it in October. However, because they spent their budget in this year, and they needed the product in this year, they wanted us to violate our payment terms of net 30 days, and not bill them until January of the next year. Facts:

- The customer was good for the money
- Cash flow wasn't an issue for my company
- The customer was willing to pay an interest fee for the 60 days of additional dating they needed for paying the bill in January, as long as it was included in the price of the product (they didn't want an interest bill, but they would pay the additional charge if it were added to the price of the product)

Therefore, I gave the customer 90 days to pay and agreed not to bill them until January. They approved the price for the product including the interest to cover the time in excess of 30 days during which they would have use of the product and not be responsible for payment. Result: win on both sides.

The alternative was to deny the order and send my customer to a competitor. In addition, the customer was very honest in their payment capabilities. Instead of demanding that they meet our 30-day payment terms, I asked why a company with their financial strength needed the extra time. A deal then became very clear.

For those who think this technique lacked ethical status because the customer's management team was being "deceived" by the arrangement, it was the management team responsible for budget approval that also approved the process we arranged.

Using Negotiation Tactics in the Workplace

We negotiate when we are hired, and we should negotiate our promotions and the objectives we will be judged on that measure our performance. Being forbidden to negotiate the metrics on which we are evaluated tells us something about the company. To use a simple example, let's consider our salary and benefits we receive when being hired. There is always a range of salaries in any job classification. Presumably the company will assess our skills and qualifications to do the job and make us an offer of employment with a compensation package commensurate with our ability to contribute to the success of the company. Believing that there will be a counter-offer, it will likely be on the low end of the range to leave room for some "give and take." (In some cases a company wants you so badly that they will blow you away with an offer you can't refuse, but in many cases, they are trying to get a bargain.)

If you employ appropriate negotiating tactics, you would research and know what the salary range is for your position. However, this is sometimes unavailable to you. The next step might be to ask what the range is for your position's title and then see where they placed you. From the employer's perspective, they might want to show you where you are in the range, indicating that being at the lower end of the range offers you room to grow in the position (you will not be limited in raises because you are at the top of the range, or alternatively, that being in the top of the range means you will be considered for a promotion sooner.)

Either way, you should find out where you are and what that means to your career. But, in addition, some employees want more vacation time than is offered in the "standard" package. You may try to negotiate more time off, with or without pay. You may be able to negotiate a salary review in 6 months rather than wait for a year. Salary may be tightly controlled in a published range, but a sign-on bonus may offset a somewhat lower salary to get you started. You may be willing to sacrifice salary for a higher incentive package. Salary and benefits are fungible and can be traded off to form a package that is best for the employee and not cost the employer any more than they expected to pay with their original offer. You have a package that works better for you, but it doesn't cost your employer anything more.

Negotiating a Promotion

What about the promotion that started our chapter? If we can't show that the promotion will create substantive value for the company, they have no motivation to promote you. So, what's in it for them? Can you split away a work group and manage a part of the business in which you are highly skilled? Why does promoting you make sense? As you consider this approach, notice that the attention is away from you and on the other party, in this case your employer. You are finding ways that create value for them rather than "selling" yourself as a candidate for promotion. This is the antidote to being accused of having (and concealing) a self-serving bias. In many cases, it is easy for your counterpart to conclude that your interests are all one-sided, and tilted to what's best for you, not the organization. If you want to defuse that accusation, then talk less about what you want and more about what the organization needs, and how you can deliver it.

Of course, if they decline your generous offer, do you have a BATNA? Is being rejected for the position going to sit well with you? Does it tell you something about the way the company and its management team think of you? Do you have an offer from another company that is willing to hire you in that same position level? As you prepare for this negotiation, there is a lot to consider. Without this pre-work you would be in the dark, groping for a reason to be promoted and then left with no process forward if you were rejected.

Power Distribution

Who has the power in the negotiation? Does it matter? Can we blunt the impact of power based with our counterpart? Clearly, when you are negotiating a salary increase or promotion with your boss, the perception is that the boss holds the power. The one who has the ability to say "no" is usually attributed with the greater share of power. However, we can lessen that power by using several tactics. First, if we downplay the power mal-distribution and appear confident, we may weaken that power bias. Second, what if it is really the employee who has the power? Replacing an employee is expensive and some skills are not found in a timely fashion. What if the employee has another job waiting for them, and they will resign if their career goals are not met? What if the employee becomes disappointed in a rejection and it affects their performance? It should be obvious that the one with power would be ill-advised to wield it with impunity, regardless of whether it is the employee or the employer.

In fact, when it is clear that one party has no power in the negotiation, and they know it, they have nothing to lose and may act in unpredictable ways. So the restraint of power may be a more beneficial instrument than the display of power.

Neither is it a good idea to ignore power that is identified by the lines of an organization chart. We might agree that ignoring the position power of the company's CEO would be folly.

Either side of the negotiation can mitigate power resident with their counterpart if they have planned properly. For the employee, having a "Plan B" if their request is not approved gives them some ultimate power. The employer can protect against employee power by having a strong succession plan for critical positions. Many managers disregard the need for succession planning because they don't think it is an important management tool. They are short-term thinkers and believe that everyone is replaceable. Well, some are more easily, inexpensively, and quickly replaceable than others, and it would be wise for managers to reserve their position power by having a backup for their employees' externally generated options.

Negotiating Objectives

Some of the more important metrics in our work lives are those objectives we are charged with accomplishing during the year. In most organizations there is a top-down management structure that goes from the company mission to the strategic directives, and finally flowing down to the operational objectives each employee must accomplish to meet the company's overall goals, such as a 10% improvement in profitability or a 3% improvement in employee satisfaction. We can't just waive our magic wand and make that happen. We need to develop and execute activities to support those goals and charge our employees with performing those activities successfully. If we don't do our jobs well and meet our departmental metrics, it is unlikely we will meet our company's goals.

Employee Satisfaction Activities

For instance, if we want to improve employee satisfaction, then we might set a goal of establishing an employee recognition program which is highly correlated with employee satisfaction. What are we looking to reward? Who decides? What are the rewards? How often is the recognition awarded? If this is a new program, what are reasonable goals? It is a process that should be driven by employees.

Whether a company calls it a negotiation process or not, this kind of give-and-take is a necessary part of engaging employees in the decision-making process, without which there is no buy-in from employees. Anytime an employee is simply told what to do, they have been denied authority in the process and they have no responsibility for the outcome.

Style

Negotiation isn't just about having the facts. And, here is where many negotiators slip up. We can say the right things in the wrong way and anger our counterpart in ways that prevent the message from ever getting through. Many of us find that when working with some people, we are not inclined to come to agreement, even when our disagreeable posture is detrimental to ourselves. We just don't like the person and therefore, we balk at anything they say.

In some instances, I have found that I am keenly aware that my emotions are controlling my logic and I have reached out to a colleague or my boss to discuss a situation. A third party opinion can look at a situation dispassionately and offer advice to help you through the mental block you may have for a person and get to your real interests. We all have to work through difficult people or those we simply don't like to achieve our goals. However, there is another method we can use to step away from the situation and look at the process from a more objective perspective. It is called "going to the balcony", and it is described in the book 3D Negotiation by Lax and Sebenius.

Going to the Balcony

This is a process that fans of Shakespearean plays are familiar with. Usually somewhere in the play, a character will perform a soliloquy while up on a "balcony" overlooking the stage. While the other characters are still on the stage in clear view and within earshot, they are in shadow and the words of the balcony character, who is in the spotlight, are meant for the audience alone; they cannot be heard by the other characters on the stage. This feeling of physical isolation gives the character a chance to voice their plans and heartfelt sentiments, and for the audience to consider the happenings on stage in the context of the thoughts divulged by our "balcony-speaker", without the confusion of interference from anyone else in the play. It is a secret we are being told, which informs our views of what we have seen up to this point, and sets the direction and our understanding of events in future scenes.

In negotiation, when we are caught up in the moment and may be driven more by emotion than logic (remember that a negotiation is intended to deliver a result and not primarily a "feeling"), we should step back from the action, so to speak, and "go to the balcony" where we can review the process and try to see it as others may see it. How would this negotiation appear to others? Am I being reasonable? Is this going the way I originally intended? Should I change my tactics to achieve a better result based on what I've learned so far? We might call it taking a break, but it is more than a delay in timing to consider new information.

Going to the balcony assists us in gaining a deeper reflection about the process, but more importantly, how the positions might be viewed by a dispassionate outsider. We don't need that outsider to be a resource to us, we can do it alone, as long as we can be objective about something that has us emotionally connected as well as intellectually engaged. Once we can see ourselves and our positions objectively, and we are happy with the way others might view us, then we can resume our negotiations without the burden of emotional feelings skewing our decisions. When we are mad, especially, we are subject to making poor decisions, (it's the "cut off your nose to spite your face" analogy) which we may avoid by "going to the balcony."

Does My Personality Get in the Way?

No, there is nothing wrong with your personality. Everyone can be a good negotiator regardless of our natural personality if we pay attention to our approach to bargaining. This is more of a process that may make you more successful under most situations. If you tend to be a hard-charging, get a win at all costs kind of negotiator, it will work sometimes and not others. If matched with a counterpart who is comfortable in a confrontational environment, one who can give as well as they take, this may be just what you both need to hammer out a solution. If matched with a shrinking wallflower who will cower under your tirade and give you whatever you demand just to stop the pain, you may also win (though durability may be in question.)

However, this avoider of conflict may also cut-and-run, eliminating any hope of getting to a fair deal.

As we negotiate, we learn about our counterpart. Are they timid and thoughtful or are they single-minded and forceful? Have they prepared with a result in mind or are they just feeling out the territory to see what may be possible? The more we learn about our counterpart's needs as well as their demeanor, the better prepared we are to sync our approach to a process that will resonate with our counterpart and help them get through the negotiation with a mutually beneficial result. It's not that our personality is bad, but acting in ways that facilitate a better outcome may be more beneficial at achieving our goals than always being ourselves.

As we talked about that hiring process where the employee gets what they want and the employer is indifferent to the result because it doesn't cost them more than the standard package, so too are we always looking for a mutual gain when we negotiate in any situation. So, while your personality may work just fine most of the time, it is suggested that modifying your approach depending on the needs of your counterpart will make you more successful and a person who is viewed as easy to work with. This occurs despite the fact that you got what you wanted all along.

Help Them Get What They Want, Too

Whose negotiation is it, anyway? Why should I be responsible for their outcome? If they can't handle the heat, why are they in this kitchen? These are all good questions rooted in the presumption that we are splitting a pizza. The more they get, the less I get. It's that simple. I'm in it to win, not to give them what they want. And, when it comes to a pizza, if you want 5 slices of an 8 slice pie, then they get 3. None of this 4 and 4 for us!

However, many negotiations are not like the fixed pie of splitting a pizza, nor are they one-dimensional, straight line and fixed process all the time. In the scenario with our sisters and the orange scenario, one orange could serve two purposes, and in the 90 day payment terms for my customer, one size doesn't necessarily fit all when it comes to fulfilling a client's needs and your policies. This means that even if your counterpart is not as prepared as you are, and if they are not familiar with the style of mutually beneficial outcomes, you can help them achieve their goals as long as you can also get what you want.

This is reflective of a negotiation between management and labor. Say that we are management and we are in a tough negotiation. One of the exercises we can go through is to "walk a mile in their shoes". This is a common theme and one that is taught in the Harvard "Program on Negotiation" courses. In this case we are challenged to take our counterpart's role and explain to our union membership the agreement we just penned with management. What is so good about it? How will it benefit our membership? Why didn't we get more? If we can't make a good argument for our counterpart, then they can't either. How do we help them achieve a gain that meets their fundamental requirements without giving up those results that are "must have's" to us? We're not being soft; we're trying to achieve a mutually beneficial agreement. If we get what we want, why would we care what they get? The intention isn't to inflict pain unnecessarily; it is to reach our goal.

The take-away from the sisters with the orange case is that a compromise does not always result in the best outcome for either party. There are many times when both sides can have their way because the factors that are most important to them are mutually exclusive. Each can have what they want if they are willing to engage in principled negotiation. This entails exploring their interests rather than their positions, which implies that both parties investigate the needs of the other party and try to work in concert to solve the problem together. In this way we may find that the benefits to both parties increase the size of the pie to 10 slices. Even if we have equal shares, we still get our 5 slices, but we must also be comfortable with our counterpart also getting their 5 slices. By our argument, our goal was to get 5 slices. Who cares that they also got a good deal?

I was the General Manager of a company that had a union shop. This union was always asking for something, whether it was a modification of our contract or a benefit for their members that wasn't specifically spelled-out in the contract. Almost all of the time, the answer from me was, "we can take that up at our next contract negotiation." However, on one occasion I was approached by the employees directly. They were having trouble with the overtime process that was documented in the union contract. Now that they were working to this new process that they said they wanted, it wasn't as flexible as they had hoped.

All employees had daily access to our management team, but in this instance they asked to have a formal meeting between their union shop steward, our service manager, and me to discuss a change in their union contract dealing with overtime scheduling. They presented their case well and we agreed to meet the next day to continue the discussion. The service manager was indifferent to the process of overtime scheduling as long as he had complete flexibility to send out a team anytime a customer required service. However, we had spent quite a bit of time reviewing the current process that the union wanted at our last negotiation, which we knew met our needs. So, we agreed to meet with the union steward again.

My charge to the union steward was to meet with his membership and 1) develop a method that they liked better, 2) not increase our cost of service, 3) maintain the same or better customer service, 4) not meet on company time, and 5) make sure that the union business manager is in agreement with the proposed new scheme. We would give a trial to any process they wanted that met those conditions, and if they didn't like it better, we would revert to our current method.

In this case, the union had free reign to dream up an overtime process that worked for them, and we had control over our cost and customer satisfaction. I didn't care that they got something that was good for them as long as we had what management wanted also. The result was that they came up with a good plan that they liked better. We wrote an addendum to the union contract. They were happier, we were indifferent, and life moved on.

Be Able to Explain Your Positions and Interests Convincingly

No one likes to negotiate with someone they don't trust. You simply can't count on anything they say. It is critically important that we maintain our integrity throughout a negotiation, and the quickest way to lose it would be to say something that we can't support. So, if you go to your boss and ask for that promotion, you should be prepared to answer the question "why?" If you don't have a compelling reason for the boss to promote you, he/she won't have one either. By the same token, when you are negotiating with someone, it is useful to ask "why is that important to you," or "please help me understand how that benefits you without being a disadvantage to me?" We are trying to see if there is an underlying theme or truth to the argument, or if our counterpart is just playing a game to see what they can get, or what your reaction would be.

If you are asked about your request for a promotion or a raise and you say, "well, it's about time, don't you think?", then this is indicative of a lack of understanding. What is the benefit to the company? How will it improve the organization? If the boss thought that "it was about time", then they might have thought of it before you brought it to their attention. When anyone puts forth a proposal, it should be supported with a valid reason in order for it to be credible. No one wants to negotiate against a fictitious offer that is suddenly withdrawn because it was never serious.

For example, you are negotiating wages with the union and they ask for $45 an hour in base wage for an unskilled worker. When you ask why, the only reason given is, "we thought it was a good place to start." It would be unreasonable to use that $45 figure as a benchmark to begin wage negotiations. Given this scenario, we lose faith that anything our counterpart says is rational. If faced with this tactic, it is better to ask for our counterpart to defend this position, and if it is not defensible, ask that the offer be amended. It is inappropriate to let them say "well, we made an offer, what is your offer?" This gives in to the tactic and causes you to effectively negotiate against your own prior position. Do not permit a counterpart to make ridiculous offers rather than take the process seriously. Respect for the process of negotiation is a requirement to enter the bargaining to begin with. Unruly people who try to bully their counterparts with unreasonable offers should be redirected in their approach or replaced.

Anchoring

Let's not confuse this unreasonable offer with a negotiation tactic called "anchoring". Anchoring is a way to set a high (or low) expectation in your counterpart's thinking by going to the extreme end of a range. If you are looking to negotiate a compensation package you might have information about 5 of your friends who are employed and take the very best benefits from each to begin the negotiation with your prospective employer. This may backfire, but if pressed you can honestly say that company X has a starting salary of $55,000 and company Y has 3 weeks of vacation to start, and company Z offers a 10% match for employees' 401k retirement plans, despite the fact that no company offers all these benefits in combination. It is a fictitious proposition that sets the tone for bargaining to start. Research shows that the psychological impact of anchoring is effective at driving the final settlement in the direction of the anchor, if it doesn't end the negotiation immediately because it is perceived as unreasonable. Care must be taken when using any extreme tactic. There is a chance that it will be viewed as insulting or too far out of a rational range to even consider a counteroffer.

Who Should Make the First Offer?

Should you jump in aggressively and make the first offer to get things started, or wait for your counterpart to make the first offer? Those who jump in are making a point that they want to control the negotiation. It sends a signal to the other party and attempts to set the tone that you have the most power in the process. However, since we always want to learn more about our counterpart's interests to help us formulate a mutually beneficial deal, we will gain more insight if our counterpart is permitted, and encouraged to start with the first offer. Unless we have planned to use a tactic of anchoring, which we have already indicated might back-fire on us, we want to be reasonable in our approach. We will never get more than our first offer, so it is a potential loss to us if we place the first offer on the table. If it is uncomfortable for you to do anything but to make the first offer, a good place to start requires that you have knowledge of an acceptable range, and then place the high (or low, depending on your interest in the negotiation) end of the range on the table with justification for that offer. If you are coerced into putting your best offer on the table immediately, you will give up any potential upside and will probably have to agree to a lower than anticipated result.

How Does This Mesh With Your Career Aspirations?

If we go back to that promotion you want, you might make an appointment with your boss and simply ask for the promotion. That is the equivalent of making the first offer. Of course, you are prepared with all the reasons why you should be promoted. But, what would happen if you made that same appointment and asked your boss about his/her perception of your career path? In effect, you are placing the responsibility of making the first offer on your boss. They may ask why you want to know at this time, or ask you what your interests are, but that would be shifting the responsibility of making the first offer back to you. Try to resist the temptation of blurting out your intentions for a promotion until you can gain insight into their thinking of your career with the company.

This advice is at odds with those who believe that a direct approach is best to get what you want. After all, your boss doesn't know what is on your mind. Bosses are not mind readers! Go after what you want! Be aggressive. They like people who know what they want and work to get it. You've worked hard, now go for it.

Neither one of these tactics differ in their desire for the same end result. They differ in approach. Some people are more comfortable with a direct "in-your-face" approach and some aren't. What if you learn that you are not thought of as "promotion-ready" by the company? Which approach would be better in that circumstance? What if your aggressive style is not appreciated by your boss? Might it hurt your chances of getting that promotion if your style is counter to the company culture? Once again, if you do your homework and try to learn at each step along the way, you may end up with a better result.

Relationship Value

As an employee, you work in a group of peers and you work for someone who is your boss. And, these work relationships work both ways. When we come in to work tomorrow, we have to interact with those same people regardless of the topics we discussed today. So, maintaining relationships is important. Tough negotiations with your boss about starting salary might taint your working relationship in the future. For that reason, many companies have all negotiations at hiring go through the Human Resources department. It is also why sports figures have tricky negotiations conducted by their agent.

Think of negotiating with someone with whom you will never see again. While this is not a guarantee, you may assume that you will not see a used car salesman in the future, so you can assume a rather aggressive posture. But, if relationships really matter in the future, your approach may have to be different, both on the employee and the employer side. Maintaining good relationships serves several purposes. First, it makes working with your counterpart more pleasant after the negotiation and second, it gives you the reputation as someone who people would like to engage in negotiations in the future. Who would want to willingly negotiate with someone who was insulting, made them mad, took advantage of them, or someone who totally vanquished them in a prior bargaining session? And, how many times have we come through a negotiation only to find that what we thought we agreed to was immediately being violated by our counterpart? This reflects an agreement that lacks durability. We are often reminded that an agreement or contract is only worth the paper it's written on, that the true test of a settlement is based on the willingness of the participants to live out the terms and spirit of the agreement. Maintaining good relationships during the negotiation can support durability in the outcomes. The process of principled negotiation and cooperation can set the stage for future success at the negotiation table.

Perception vs. Facts

When we disagree with someone, it is often the case that two people can look at the same event and come away with entirely different views. Occasionally, there is more than one way to interpret what happened, and other times one person did not process the information correctly, and they have an incorrect view of the "facts". When we negotiate with a counterpart, we are confronted with differences in perception about issues that can be perplexing. How can two groups working together see things so differently? Perhaps it's the lens with which each party views life, such as the obvious differences in position between union and management.

However one looks at the situation, even if their perception is not supported by facts, their perception is their reality and it must be treated with respect. Why do you believe that is the case? What evidence can you provide that would help me understand your position? What exactly did you see? How do you interpret that paragraph?

So, we have two considerations. One is the scenario represented when our counterpart is not aware of the facts. In this case, our job is to present the facts in order to correct their view and thereby change their position, because it is their incorrect knowledge that is driving the conflict. In the second instance, the facts may be known but our counterpart has an incorrect interpretation of the facts, thereby driving a perception that gives rise to the conflict. In this case, and since their perception is their reality, we should try to change their perception to align with the facts. Let's also remember that even as skilled negotiators, we may be mistaken in our views. It is just as incumbent on us to be open to new information given to us during negotiation and permit our minds to be modified to arrive at a meaningful result consistent with the facts. It is not easy for many people to admit that they are wrong in their perception, or that their "facts" were wrong, especially when in the heat of battle. We are essentially admitting that our preparation was incomplete or in error. Since our positions and negotiating strategy depended on our understanding of the facts, we are pushed back in our plans. But, admitting you need to consider the new information presented is a very good posture to take. The new information may be altogether incorrect, but if it piques your interest it is better to consider it right away.

One way to do that is to regroup and call a time-out while the new infor-mation is considered. Use the time to confirm or reject the new information and don't come back to the negotiation table until you have reformulated your plan to incorporate the new "facts".

We will discuss the perils of our human condition to selectively process new information later in the book, however, the central point is "when we encounter information that is opposite to our belief, we ignore it and jus-tify that by thinking the new information must be wrong." As we consider new information given to us as we negotiate, we must be keenly aware that our inclination would be to ignore its salient points, while the information likely forms the central theme of our counterparts' argument. Reconciling the two will be difficult but important to resolving the conflict.

From the Management Perspective

We have been running this argument as if the employee is the only one who needs to assume a negotiating posture in the organization. But, in reality that is far from the truth. Leadership may be defined in many ways and be associated with many attributes, but in its essence, leadership is the skill of getting things done through other people. Dwight D. Eisenhower is quoted as saying "Leadership is the art of getting someone else to do something you want done because he wants to do it." It is the application of soft skills that results in influencing a person's behavior. This is the same process that we find in any negotiation. We are trying to persuade someone to give us something that we want with techniques that mimic successful leadership profiles.

It is those soft skills that can make the major difference between an effective leader and someone who is not respected by their employees. Both can say "no" to an employee, but they manage to convey the message in different ways. How many times have we been accused of misusing language in a way that prompts the response "it's not what you said, it's how you said it!" No one likes to receive an insensitive message. Good leaders instinctively know how to communicate in a way that considers the feelings of the recipient. Those who become good leaders learn this skill along the way, but when placed under pressure, that quick response that lacks sensitivity may come out. It is when everyone is under stress that good leaders can promote calm and understanding. Conveying a bad message or persuading people to do something that they don't want to do, or find distasteful, is the mark of a good leader and the mark of a good negotiator.

CHAPTER 7: LINKING EMPLOYEE SATISFACTION TO CUSTOMER SATISFACTION

"Management works in the system; Leadership works on the system." Stephen R. Covey

Optimizing Employee Performance

Let's work on the following premise. Employees want to satisfy customers. Furthermore, employees want to be gainfully employed, being neither too busy nor not busy enough. The more effectively our employees work, the happier they are and the happier our customers will be. Yet, there are few systems that optimize the time and effort of our employees. Most managers give employees work, and then keep piling it on until they have overworked their employees who then complain to get some relief, or the employee quits.

This is a poor method from several aspects. First, slow employees do less work than fast employees, which carries with it an inherent unfairness that is recognized by the better employees. Next, since most workers have a wide range of work to do, and there is a random arrival of jobs, it is impossible to have full utilization from any employee. This is a serious problem and it is often dealt with poorly by management. For instance, an efficient employee who has just completed a job is waiting for another job to come along, and is using the time to do some planning for future projects. While thinking, he is perceived as loafing.

This chapter presents results of an analysis that optimizes the use of multi-channel service providers to reduce the wait time that customers must endure before a service can be performed. Despite the fact that airlines and supermarkets have made use of quick check-out lines to speed the delivery of service, many companies do not implement multiple service channels and therefore do not enjoy the benefits of dedicated, multi-channel service to improve employee productivity, employee satisfaction, and customer satisfaction.

In fact, the results of this work show those customers with long-term project needs and those with short-term service needs both benefit substantially by dedicating some portion of the service providers to only short-term projects. This is counterintuitive, since it is natural to believe if we take someone away from the long projects to "fight fires", it will delay the long projects. This chapter shows that dedicated services can shorten the wait time for short and long-term projects.

Rationale

As an academic and consultant, it is common for me to see customer satisfaction surveys that claim "service takes too long". Using a simple reassignment of service staff, a company can substantially decrease the wait time that all customers experience when they request service. This is the major point. Reassigning only a few people to dedicated service for short-term problems can decrease the wait time dramatically for both long and short-term projects. The method works best at companies that have a variety of service problems and project opportunities; service that is varied in the time it takes to complete the task. For instance, the IT department that needs to introduce a new report as well as deal with giving new users passwords.

This technique is not a new concept. Supermarkets use quick check-out lines to good advantage. The value of this analysis is to broaden the application to a wider range of service organizations and to highlight that it is possible to distribute jobs to your employees that can do wonders for your customer satisfaction metrics.

Background

When working with clients, it is often the case that lots of thought goes into the tactical delivery of a service, but little effort is expended on the process of service delivery, in other words, how to best utilize the employee's productive time. As an example, the IT department of a company has to provide many different types of support to their internal customers. They fix printers, unlock computers, recover files, develop new reports, and introduce product upgrades or roll out new programs, to name a few. These services differ in many ways, but a distinguishing feature of these services is the amount of time it takes to complete each of the tasks. If it takes a technician 15 minutes to unlock a computer or 2 hours to fix a printer problem, those customers do not expect to wait 2 days until they are served. The urgency of the job often is proportional to the time it will take to complete the job.

A second case comes from the engineering development field. One company was routinely approached by influential customers who needed simple engineering changes to specify the bill of materials for short-run products. The manufacturing company was not anxious to offer this service since it meant taking valuable engineering time out of long-term projects to sell low-volume products as a courtesy to its customer. When a company relies on development of engineered products that will enjoy high volumes, this is not always a welcome request. But, when a good customer (read that "high margin") wants engineering time, while it is not always convenient to break into another project's schedule, it is done. This is another example of a short-term need infringing on the labor allocation for longer-term projects.

Dealing with these conflicts usually means "fighting fires" because planning for unspecified problems that arise randomly is not easy. And, as with challenges of this type, if we can find a way to do it efficiently, we can increase the satisfaction level of our customers as well as our employees. It is natural to believe that taking resources away from the long-term projects will compromise our commitments to those activities. This chapter demonstrates that by segregating service channels into dedicated short-term service and dedicated long-term projects, we can improve the performance of both. The motivation for employees is that it will be rare that an employee will be bored on the job, and equally unlikely that they will be overworked.

The Model

The solution to our dilemma requires more than simply prioritizing incoming jobs. Prioritization leads to favoritism. No one likes to wait for a service. It is imperative that a solution which improves the waiting experience for short-term service jobs must not disadvantage the wait for long-term projects.

At the same time, we want to minimize cost, which means adding no more labor content than that which is absolutely necessary.

Texts concentrate on improving the waiting line experience for customers by either reducing the service time (get more work out of the existing workforce) or increasing the number of service channels (throw money at the problem and add more service technicians).

An effective solution must incorporate a decision criterion to optimize performance of the system of jobs, while still incorporating prioritization, if necessary. The solution must also account for the cost of the operations, and minimize it for the method to be accepted.

Waiting Line Models

One way we could address this problem is to see it as a waiting line (queue). These are often modeled with Poisson arrival patterns. The Poisson arrival distribution is particularly appropriate for service jobs since they show up randomly and while we can predict how many we will receive each year, we can never predict exactly when the next one will arrive.

The Poisson process shows that the time between events is distributed in an exponential fashion. Service times are also modeled using an exponential distribution. This weighs shorter service times more heavily than longer service times. Other models exist, and if your situation would dictate a more specific arrival or service distribution to fit your needs, it would be best to modify your analysis to incorporate that information.

The exponential distribution looks like this:

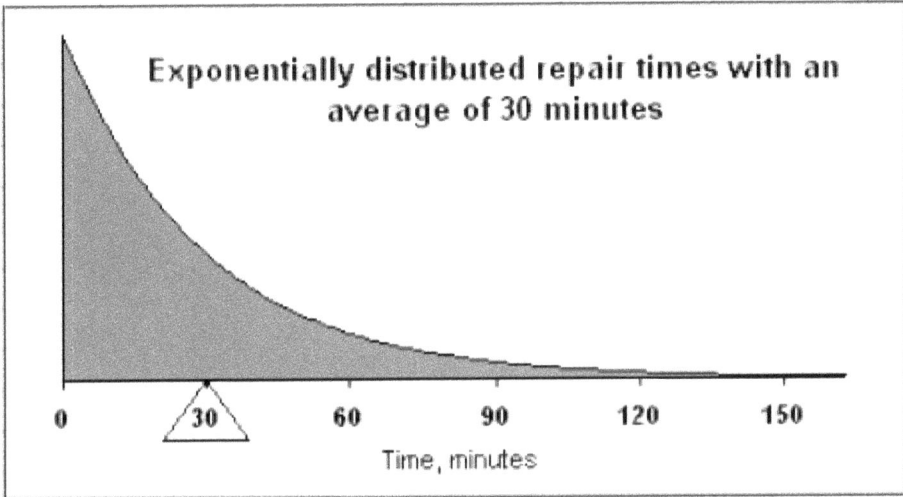

Exponentially distributed repair times with an average of 30 minutes

While arrivals and service (from a practical perspective) do not have their highest probability at zero time, an instruction to "reboot your computer" comes as close as possible. Some arrivals come in "two at a time," and some service is provided as a simple instruction so as to make this model appropriate for many situations.

Whatever the assumptions are, our motivation is to improve service to our customers while at the same time making the best use of our employee's time. The model presented here proposes to segregate service to dedicated providers based on the length of time needed for each service.

The next figure shows the traditional queuing system with one waiting line and multiple servers. Consider that all customers are directed to wait in this line regardless of their specific need for service.

Typical Multi-Server Queue

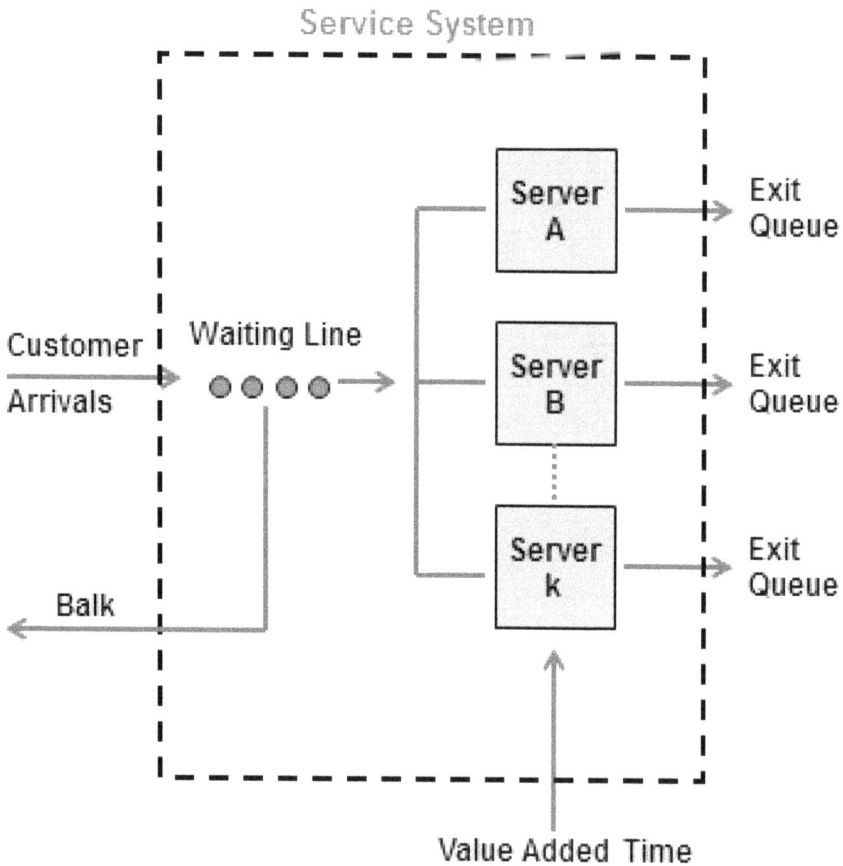

Figure 1

The figure below shows the proposed model of having two waiting lines, one for jobs of short duration and one for jobs of long duration. Customers would be directed to either the short-job line or the long-job line immediately upon entering the queue.

Proposed Multi-Server Queue

Service System

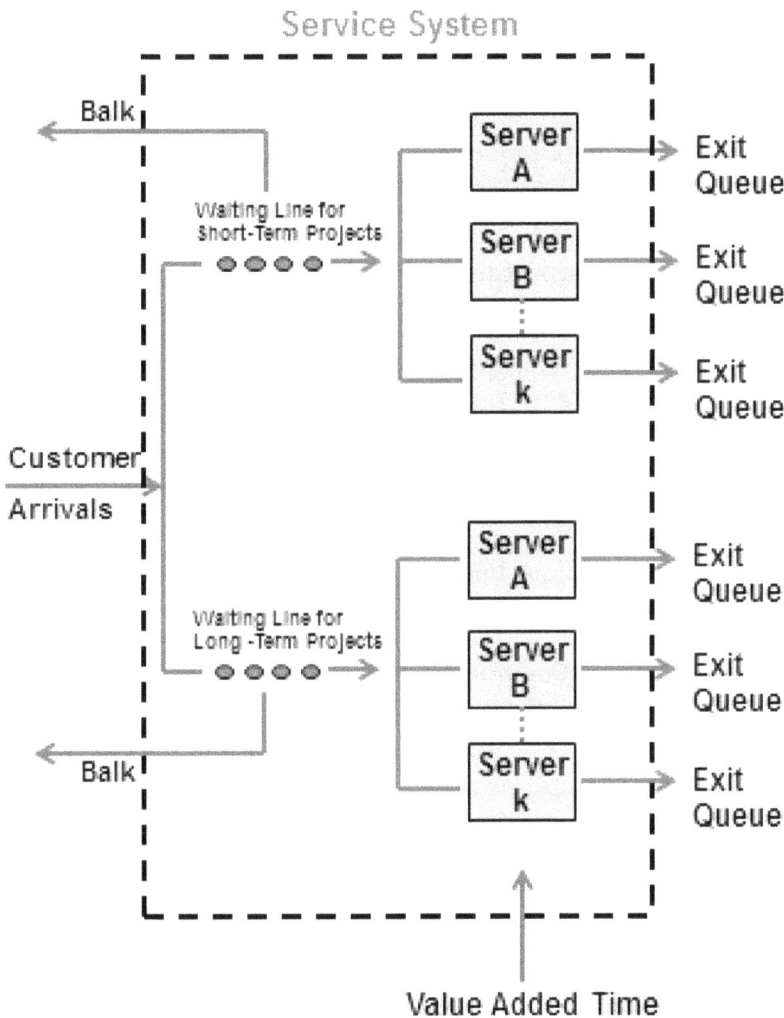

Figure 2

Case Example

Let's say we have a service department that handles 200 jobs a month. Of these jobs, 150 are short jobs, each taking an average of 2 hours to complete.

The remaining 50 jobs take 41.6 hours to complete on average. Then, in a month, we would need 2380 hours to complete these jobs, and that translates into about 14 employees, all of whom work at near 100% utilization. While this is an unrealistic assumption, any upper limit on employee utilization will work in this analysis. You simply must add the appropriate number of employees to cover the workload, given the discrepancy between the hours paid to employees and the hours of work received.

This is the only input data we need to completely analyze a waiting line model for this service department. However, these service times and arrival times are averages and not a constant rate for every job. There is a highly non-linear pattern to the arrival and service distributions. Think of sitting in your favorite frozen yogurt shop and watching the arriving customer pattern.

Customers arrive in pairs, sometimes a few pairs at a time, and sometimes there may be a group of 8 that comes in at once. The average number of arrivals does not fully describe the dynamics of the waiting line in the shop. Similar arguments hold for the service pattern, where some customers want a simple dessert and others want one with all the toppings requiring more value-added in service. Waiting lines build and decline in size as the day progresses, and for that reason we look at the probabilistic nature of the queue.

The first step is to analyze this problem as if all jobs went into a single queue as shown in Figure 1, regardless of the time it takes to complete a job. It is a single queue with 14 service channels. If we assume that the average time to complete a job comprised of 75% short and 25% long jobs is 11.9 hours, then the single queue, multi-channel service model gives us the following results (for an M/M/14 model in the Kendall notation):

- Probability that a customer has to wait = 95.0%
- Average wait time until service is provided = 69.4 hours

Imagine that you are served by this department and you have a locked computer. You would have to wait (on average) 69.4 hours until someone could address your need. That might not be an unexpected wait time for someone who has a job that takes 40 hours to complete, but a simple service ticket really should be attacked in a time that responds to the urgency of the situation.

The Link to Customer Satisfaction

When conducting satisfaction interviews with customers of my consulting clients, two of the most common complaints about service are, "it takes too long to get anything done", and "we need better communications". These are often related. The likely refrain is, "It's fine once they get to it" and "I would be more understanding of the delays if they would keep me informed as to their progress." Customers want it when they want it, how they want it, and where they want it. Since this is not always realistic, and customers know that, the closer we can come to meeting customer's needs, the higher their level of satisfaction. Everyone knows that a 2 hour job takes 2 hours to complete. That is the only "value-added" time. And, it is very annoying to wait for 2 hours to get it started. This is wasted time, or time that does not add value. Cutting out the wasted time means getting "lean," and that is the benefit of optimizing waiting lines.

The Improved Model

We never want our waiting line to grow large enough that customers must wait so long that it entices them to exit the queue, an action called "balking." When a customer balks, they arbitrage their satisfaction by finding another supplier to serve their needs, and in this way, you have encouraged your customer to become acquainted with your competitor, or disobey policy. If a customer can't balk because they are captive in terms of being required to use internal service providers, then they become disgruntled. They make demands and complain loudly to achieve satisfaction because they are dissatisfied by the base service that you provide. Either way, making customers wait is never desirable, and we should do whatever is financially feasible to minimize the wait time for our customers. This results in improved customer satisfaction and better respect for the employee, which are very desirable outcomes for a service department.

The question then is, would it be better to provide two distinct service lines (potentially, each with multiple service channels) to address the long wait times resultant from our mixed-service, single waiting line model?

The intent is to meet the following objectives:

- Minimize the probability that a customer has to wait
- Minimize the wait time before service can be provided
- No increase in the number of service providers
- No pressure to improve the service time
- Choose a staffing mix that keeps employees busy

Under these assumptions, the model of Figure 2 applies. It is two separate queues, one with an M/M/1+ Kendall designation for the short jobs and the other with an M/M/13- designation for the long jobs. This is analyzed as a parametric study to assess the best mix of the number of providers for the different service channels. In addition, the second parameter is the percentage of short jobs that are given to the short job employees. For instance, instead of 14 providers in one waiting line (arrivals), the model is analyzed as a series of cases that consider providers in different combinations between service lines as follows:

- 1 server in the short-job line, 13 servers in the long-job line, (1, 13)
- 2 servers in the short-job line, 12 servers in the long-job line, (2, 12)
- 3 servers in the short-job line, 11 servers in the long-job line, (3, 11)
- 4 servers in the short-job line, 10 servers in the long-job line, (4, 10)

The reason for considering these cases is to evaluate the impact that they have on the utilization of each set of employees (we don't want one group sitting around with lots of time on their hands, while the other group is working every minute of every day). Also, we want to see how much work we should transfer to each of the queues to minimize the wait for all customers. Notice that all these options use only 14 total employees.

In our case we have 150 short jobs and 50 long jobs. When we move (say) 20% of the short-term jobs to its dedicated queue, we are shifting 30 of the 150 short-term jobs to that dedicated queue leaving 170 jobs (120 short and 50 long jobs) in the queue that handles mixed jobs.

Why does this help us solve the problem? Because, the long jobs block up our system. With 50 long jobs entering the system per month, and each long job taking 41.6 hours to complete on average, if four long jobs come in on any particular day, that will dedicate four employees to those jobs, and with around 12 long jobs entering the system every week, all the service employees might be working on those long jobs at any one time, leaving no service employees to work on the short jobs. Therefore, dedicating employees to the short jobs only, gives them the ability to get those completed, and still leave most of the employees free to work on the long jobs.

Results of the Analysis

There are five dimensions to our problem.

- How long is too long for a customer to wait for service?
- How many people should we dedicate to short-term jobs?
- What percentage of the short-term jobs should we shift to those dedicated workers?
- What is the probability of a wait and how long would that wait be? We might have a high probability of waiting, but if we only wait 15 minutes on average, then that might not be bad.
- What is the probability of an empty system? In other words, is there a high probability that workers will be idle in one queue and very busy in the other? The corollary to that is the question, have we over-utilized one group of employees giving them more work than they can handle?

Figures 3 through 6 display the results of the analysis in graphical form. We can quickly dispense with the 1, 13 model since it is very easy to over-work or under-work employees given the metrics in this example. This condition is noticed when a scenario results in an arrival rate that exceeds the service rate for that case. Logically, and on the other end of the spectrum, when 4 employees are shifted from the long-job line to the short-job line, and we shift very few jobs (say 20%) to the short-job line, there are lots of employees on the short line to handle very few jobs. At the same time, there are fewer employees on the long-job line to handle the remaining 80% of the jobs, many of which require more hours to complete. In general, whenever the probability of a wait is more than 95% or less than 5%, we can expect workers to be over-or under-worked. That means we should be deciding on the trade-offs represented by the 2, 12 model, or the 3, 11 model, or the 4, 10 model.

In our efforts to minimize the wait time for customers, we might consider matching the probability of a wait for both short and long jobs. They will take different times to complete, but getting jobs into the service channel after experiencing the same wait time probability shows no favoritism to either service request. While the benefits of matching the probability (likelihood) of waiting for the short and long projects are questionable, this gives us a good place to start our decision process. In coming to the final decision, we will use management judgment to choose the right mix of employees to handle the workload based on customer expectations and business benefits.

Figures 7 through 10 show the predicted wait time corresponding to each of these models. It is apparent that as we move short jobs to their dedicated providers, both the probability of a wait and the actual wait time decreases for both long and short job customers.

From a practical standpoint, in the 3, 11 model for instance, shifting the optimum number of jobs to the short job employees (60%), there is a 6 minute wait for a short job to be started and a 21 minute wait for a long job to be started. In the worst case for the 3, 11 model, if all 100% of the short jobs were shifted to the short job providers there would be a 33% chance that a short job would have to wait for 32 minutes, and a 1.2% chance that a long job would have to wait for 1 minute. That is a very large range over which the outcomes are all acceptable.

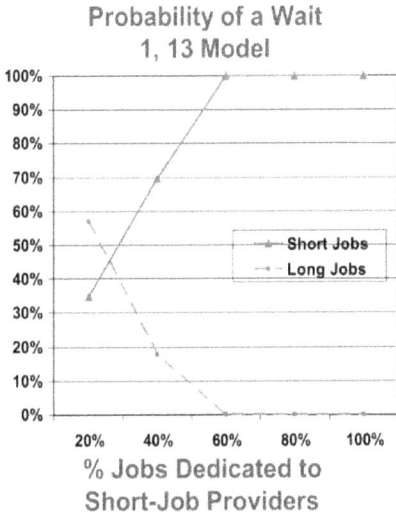

Probability of a Wait
1, 13 Model

% Jobs Dedicated to
Short-Job Providers
Figure 3

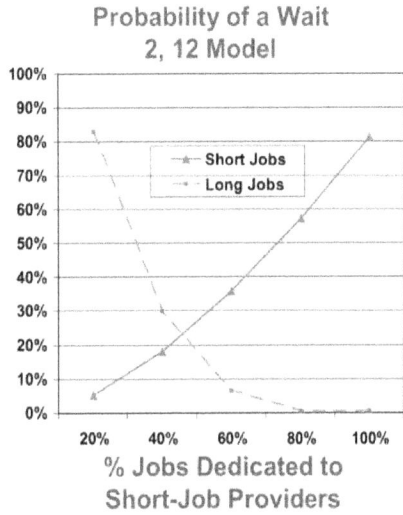

Probability of a Wait
2, 12 Model

% Jobs Dedicated to
Short-Job Providers
Figure 4

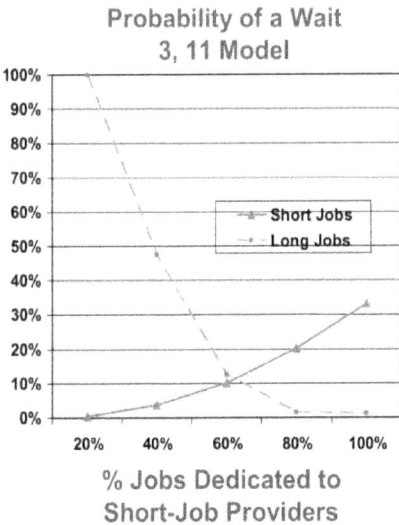

Probability of a Wait
3, 11 Model

% Jobs Dedicated to
Short-Job Providers
Figure 5

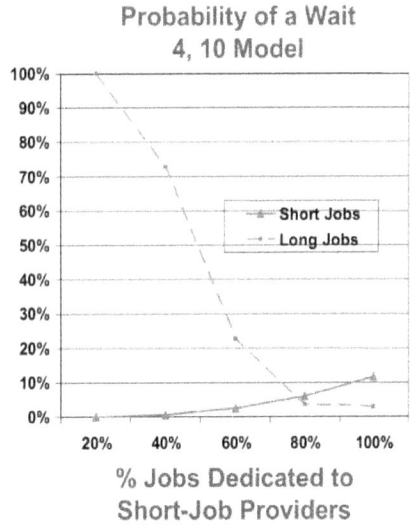

Probability of a Wait
4, 10 Model

% Jobs Dedicated to
Short-Job Providers
Figure 6

Average Wait Time (Hours) 1, 13 Model

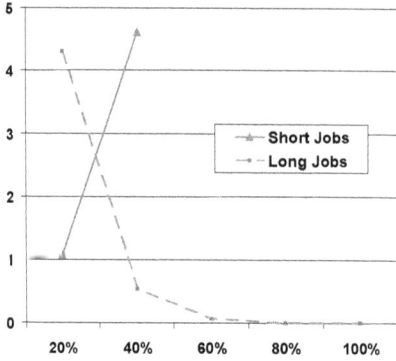

% Jobs Dedicated to
Short-Job Providers
Figure 7

Average Wait Time (Hours) 2, 12 Model

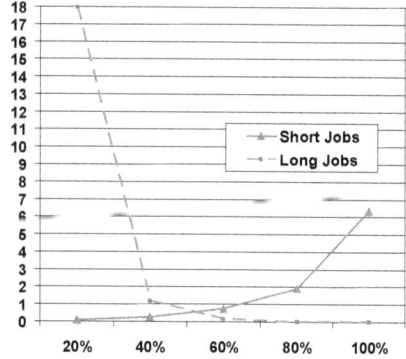

% Jobs Dedicated to
Short-Job Providers
Figure 8

Average Wait Time (Hours) 3, 11 Model

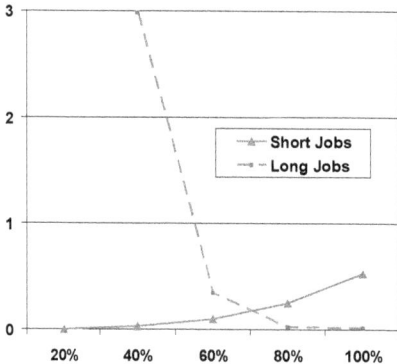

% Jobs Dedicated to
Short-Job Providers
Figure 9

Average Wait Time (Hours) 4, 10 Model

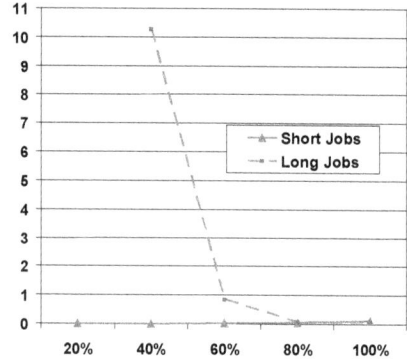

% Jobs Dedicated to
Short-Job Providers
Figure 10

The probability of a wait, the average wait time at that condition, and the probability of idle workers may be summarized as follows:

Table 1
<u>Summary of Results</u>

	2, 12 Model	3, 11 Model	4, 10 Model
Probability of a wait for either short or long jobs	25%	10%	5%
% of short jobs sent to dedicated providers	45%	60%	80%
<u>Wait time</u>			
Short jobs	25 minutes	6 minutes	3 minutes
Long jobs	60 minutes	21 minutes	5 minutes
Probability of zero <u>jobs in the queue</u>:			
Short jobs	45%	34%	24%
Long jobs	0%	0%	0%

At this point, management decision-making comes in. There are several trade-offs to consider before making the final choice of system design. First, is there some work we can give to the short-job employees when they are idle? Second, when we choose a model, does it give sufficient latitude to accommodate normal variation in arrival rate without under-or over-working any employees?

If you want flexibility to give somewhat more work to the short-job employees, then it is best to leave a little slack in their schedule, and choose the 3, 11 model, moving 60% of the short jobs into that dedicated queue. Another choice that offers similar benefits, albeit less flexibility is the 4, 10 model, moving 80% of the short jobs into that dedicated queue.

End Note

In all these models, the employees who are working on the long projects never get a break. They are mostly utilized at full capacity principally because the short-term jobs represent only 300 average hours per month out of the 2380 hours of incoming work per month. The natural question is, "why do we need 3 or 4 employees (21% to 29% of the workforce) dedicated to those short jobs when they represent only 12.6% of the work?" The reason is that we are trying to serve customers with as little wait time as is rational, and with a Poisson arrival rate that represents a non-uniform distribution, if it so happens that 4 jobs enter the system at one time, the wait time is not only determined by the ability of employees to service the account, it is affected also by the probability of a high arrival volume that is the nature of the distribution. For this reason, we need a larger number of servers dedicated to the short jobs, because while they represent only 12% of the work hours, they represent 75% of the volume of jobs entering the system.

As we choose the best alternative, any of the cases studied resulted in substantially improved wait times for both short and long jobs. Customers will take note that you get to their work more quickly, in a matter of minutes, not hours or days. That leads to improved customer satisfaction.

Every case is different, and each company should perform this analysis using their own metrics that describe the service they provide. A simple waiting line model is easy to simulate and find the right combination of labor force and number of jobs to shift to dedicated service providers. It is the dedication of service providers to the short jobs that brings the benefits. It is only an application of the "express service" model we all know.

Waiting line models can be found in any text on quantitative methods. I used "Quantitative Methods for Business," Anderson, Sweeney, Williams, 9th Ed. 2004, Thomson South-Western.

The equations that describe a multi-channel system are:

Operating Characteristics

The following formulas can be used to compute the steady-state Operating characteristics for multiple-channel waiting lines, where

λ = the mean arrival rate for the system
μ = the mean service rate for *each* channel
k = the number of channels

1. The probability that no units are in the system:

$$P_0 = \frac{1}{\sum_{n=0}^{k-1} \frac{(\lambda/\mu)^n}{n!} + \frac{(\lambda/\mu)^k}{k!}\left(\frac{k\mu}{k\mu - \lambda}\right)}$$

2. The average number of units in the waiting line:

$$L_q = \frac{(\lambda/\mu)^k \lambda\mu}{(k-1)!(k\mu - \lambda)^2} P_0$$

3. The average number of units in in the system:

$$L = L_q + \frac{\lambda}{\mu}$$

4. The average time a unit spends in the waiting line:

$$W_q = \frac{L_q}{\lambda}$$

5. The average time a unit spends in the system:

$$W = W_q + \frac{1}{\mu}$$

6. The probability that an arriving unit has to wait for serivce:

$$P_w = \frac{1}{k!}\left(\frac{\lambda}{\mu}\right)^k \left(\frac{k\mu}{k\mu - \lambda}\right) P_0$$

Table 2
1 Server for Short Jobs
13 Servers for Long Jobs

% Jobs Dedicated to Short Job Providers	Probability of a Wait		Average Wait Time (Hours)		Probability of Zero Jobs in the Queue	
	Short Jobs	Long Jobs	Short Jobs	Long Jobs	Short Jobs	Long Jobs
20%	34.9%	57.0%	1.07	4.31	65%	0%
40%	69.8%	17.9%	4.62	0.53	30.2%	0%
60%	100%	0%	*	0.06	0%	0%
80%	100%	0%	*	0	0%	0.7%
100%	100%	0%	*	0	0%	0.8%

Table 3
2 Servers for Short Jobs
12 Servers for Long Jobs

% Jobs Dedicated to Short Job Providers	Probability of a Wait		Average Wait Time (Hours)		Probability of Zero Jobs in the Queue	
	Short Jobs	Long Jobs	Short Jobs	Long Jobs	Short Jobs	Long Jobs
20%	5.2%	82.9%	0.06	17.97	70.3%	0%
40%	18.0%	29.8%	0.28	1.20	48.3%	0%
60%	35.9%	6.5%	0.75	0.14	31.3%	0.1%
80%	57.3%	0.5%	1.90	0.01	17.8%	0.7%
100%	81.3%	0.5%	6.35	0.01	6.8%	0.8%

Utilization of the short job providers exceeds 100%, and wait time builds continuously.

Table 4
3 Servers for Short Jobs
11 Servers for Long Jobs

% Jobs Dedicated to Short Job Providers	Probability of a Wait		Average Wait Time (Hours)		Probability of Zero Jobs in the Queue	
	Short Jobs	Long Jobs	Short Jobs	Long Jobs	Short Jobs	Long Jobs
20%	0.5%	100%	0	*	70.5%	0%
40%	3.7%	47.5%	0.03	2.98	49.6%	0%
60%	10.2%	12.4%	0.10	0.345	34.6%	0.1%
80%	20.1%	1.5%	0.25	0.026	23.7%	0.7%
100%	33.1%	1.2%	0.528	0.02	15.7%	0.8%

Table 5
4 Servers for Short Jobs
10 Servers for Long Jobs

% Jobs Dedicated to Short Job Providers	Probability of a Wait		Average Wait Time (Hours)		Probability of Zero Jobs in the Queue	
	Short Jobs	Long Jobs	Short Jobs	Long Jobs	Short Jobs	Long Jobs
20%	0%	100%	0	*	70.6%	0%
40%	0.6%	72.9%	0	10.26	49.8%	0%
60%	2.4%	22.7%	0.016	0.84	35.1%	0.1%
80%	6.0%	3.5%	0.046	0.075	24.6%	0.7%
100%	11.7%	3.0%	0.104	0.06	17.1%	0.8%

Utilization of the long job providers exceeds 100%, and wait time builds continuously.

CHAPTER 8: DESIGNING REWARD SYSTEMS

"Management by objectives works if you first think through your objectives. Ninety percent of the time you haven't." Peter F. Drucker

Employee Appraisal

Performance *goals* are a major contributor to employee satisfaction and to the appraisal process each organization sets up to assess employee performance. Employees who have realistic goals and achieve them in a supportive environment are happier than those who routinely miss their goals because compensation including salary, bonus, and incentive pay are all tied to meeting performance goals. This links performance goals to employee satisfaction, and the same goal setting process applies to performance goals as we used for satisfaction goals.

Appraisal Systems

Appraisal systems can fail to achieve their purpose for basically two reasons. One is an inappropriate method of assessing performance and the other is poor delivery of the process by the responsible manager.

Poor Assessment Methods

There is no one *best* method of employee performance assessment. Each company develops its own form with which to determine how well an employee performs on the job. Some are less bad than others [poor grammatical usage noted.] How should we evaluate employee performance when:

- We work in a dynamic environment where plans made early in the year may change because of circumstances, and not based on anything that is under the control of the employee?

- We can work extremely hard and smart, yet fail to meet our goals because the goals were set too high?

- No matter how hard we work, our success is dependent on the work of others inside or outside the organization, and they may fail to perform at a high level, causing us to miss our targets?

- We may be judged based on qualitative criteria open to interpretation?

- We may be judged based on trivial criteria, such as arriving at exactly 8:00 a.m. to start work?

Methods that Fail to Measure Performance that Correlates with Business Success

There are many performance appraisal systems that do not contribute to increased business success or assess employees on an objective scale. Some of these are highlighted below.

No Formal Appraisal

One such method is no performance appraisal system at all. Employees have no idea where they stand or how they rate on any objective scale. They can't use the scant verbal feedback they receive to determine whether they are performing well, they have no direction for career progression, and they do not know what they need to do to continuously improve their contributions to the company that may result in promotion. Even worse, they don't know if they will be fired tomorrow because they have no information with which to confirm or deny their fears.

Subjective Appraisals

Another performance mechanism is one that tries to measure behaviors that are superficial or subjective, such as a rating on the employee's loyalty or on-time arrival. There was a study on objective performance systems that attempted to take subjectivity out of the process. In this study, many employee behaviors were listed that may be contributory to superior performance, or alternatively to poor performance. The survey was given to managers at a large company and they were asked to rate their employees on each of these attributes, such as on-time arrival, getting work done on time, or number of sick days taken. Then, they were asked to rank their employees from best to worst.

This forced ranking system will be discussed next, but in all appraisal systems it is recognized that it is easy to distinguish the best performers and the worst performers. It is more difficult to rank the relative standing of employees in the mid-ranks, such as the two middle quartiles. This is because employees have different traits and one may be great at conceptualization but poor at planning, while another employee may be a detailed planner but not perform well at delivering results. Now our manager must decide who is a more valued employee. This is not always easy or objective when a well-rounded employee is required on the job.

Having the employees rated on the attributes and ranked from great to poor, a correlation was then performed to assess which of the characteristics were most prevalent in the best employees and which characteristics were most prevalent in the worst employees. It may not surprise you that there were some non-intuitive results that came out of that exercise. For instance, it was discovered that on-time arrival was poor in the best performing employees. These employees tended to stay late, work through lunch, or take work home with them, but they simply couldn't seem to arrive on time routinely. They were the best performers, but they didn't fit the established mold. It is clear that we need some better assessment attributes if we are to properly correlate appraisal results to performance and contribution to company success.

Forced Ranking Systems

Forced ranking systems are those where all employees in the company in each job category are ranked from highest to lowest in performance. With the wide range of job responsibilities in each category this is a subjective process. However, the purpose of forced ranking is to provide positive reinforcement, extraordinary pay raises, and promotion to the top 5% of the employees, and purge the lowest 5% of the employees each year. The theory is that by constantly replacing the lowest 5% of performers and replacing them with new recruits, you strengthen the employee pool each year.

One of the problems with this method is that employees from different departments must be inter-meshed to consolidate all employees in any employment category. So, as an example, all employees in the job title "Associate" or in wage level "5" must be placed in rank order for the company, not each department. Thus, all department managers must meet to agree on where their employees will be placed in the "overall" list. By one account given to me, this was done by screaming match since some managers were very protective of their employees. That means other managers lost out to the stronger ones, or rather their employees lost out. This is probably not the best approach to objective performance rating.

This system can be supplemented with coaching and time to recover from a poor appraisal, but it results in a lot of employee churn when added to natural attrition. A criticism of this process is that it ritualizes employee firing and sends a negative message to all employees that they won't be treated as individuals but rather their careers with the company are dependent on their ranking. If you have a personal tragedy in your family that causes you to be in a temporary professional slump, or you make a mistake, counseling may be bypassed because you are in the lowest 5% and that means firing is the company policy.

The Management by Objectives Approach to Performance Appraisal

Of the many ways to formulate an appraisal system, the best known is the "Management by Objectives" (MBO) approach. With MBO, each employee meets with their manager at planning time to discuss their specific job description and their responsibilities to deliver work consistent with the department goals for the next planning period. The flow of setting objectives usually starts at the top of the organizational ladder. This is often a process of "catch ball", meaning that the executive team scans the environment of economic indicators, customer needs, competitive landscape, financial capabilities, and operational performance that is discussed to formulate a set of high-level goals for the next year.

Graphically, it looks like this:

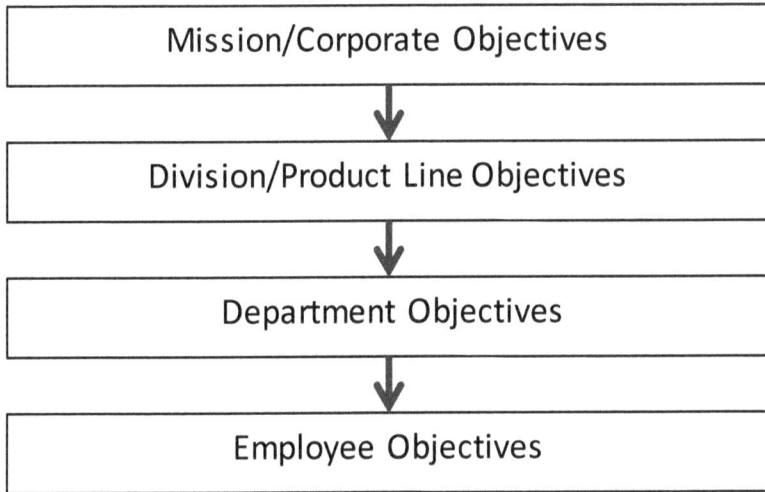

```
┌─────────────────────────────────────────────────┐
│           Mission/Corporate Objectives           │
└─────────────────────────────────────────────────┘
                        ↓
┌─────────────────────────────────────────────────┐
│          Division/Product Line Objectives         │
└─────────────────────────────────────────────────┘
                        ↓
┌─────────────────────────────────────────────────┐
│               Department Objectives               │
└─────────────────────────────────────────────────┘
                        ↓
┌─────────────────────────────────────────────────┐
│                Employee Objectives                │
└─────────────────────────────────────────────────┘
```

The corporate goals may be:

- Introduce product xyz by September in a test market
- Reach gross margin of xx% and net income of xy% of revenue
- Achieve a market share of xz% by year-end

Then, these goals are passed down to the division level where a plan is developed to meet those objectives. Included in that analysis may be:

- Capital expenditures for equipment to achieve the goal
- Human resources estimates will be planned
- Training will be estimated
- Office and production/service space will be estimated

And, if this indicates that the goals can be met, the information and details will be conveyed to the executive team. If the resources and timing are acceptable to the executive team, it is approved. If the executive team finds that any of the resources are too much for them, they should work to adjust the corporate goals to reach a level of performance they can afford. This is the "catch ball" process. The worst outcome of catchball would be a response from the executive team that all the goals must be met; however, very few of the new resources will be made available. "Do it anyway" will be the dictate. This is a highly de-motivating process. Employees were involved in the process of planning, but their recommendations were ignored. Employees are being asked to accomplish new goals with the same old resources and they have indicated that it is not possible to make that plan work. The message is that they are being set up for failure which is a poor way to motivate the workforce.

But let's say that the divisional plans are approved. Now, the division will work with the department managers to set department objectives. Once those are developed and we know what each department will be responsible for, we can review our employee's skills and determine such things as:

- New hires that will be required to supplement skill or manpower needs
- Training required to update skills for employees
- Activities that must be accomplished to reach the goals
- Resources that will be acquired to meet the goals
- Timetables for detailed activities to schedule when each of the goals will be met, and interim reviews to assure that the timetables are being met
- Planning with vendors to coordinate schedules for achieving the goals

Out of that discussion, a set of objectives will be written that define the work and deliverables each employee must achieve throughout the planning horizon (usually a year). The more quantitative the statement of activities and results expected, the less interpretation is left to the manager when the performance appraisal is delivered.

MBO appraisal forms are often paragraphs that define what has to be done by the employee and when it must be done, in detail.

It is intended to serve several purposes:

- Define the project deliverables to protect the employee from ad hoc additions or changes by the manager or anyone else in the organization

- Define the project deliverables to protect the company from having the employee deny that a deliverable was on their agenda
- Provide enough granularity in activity deadlines to determine when a project is on schedule or falling behind, so adjustments can be made

This is not to say that new objectives can't be added at any time, or that objectives can't be modified at any time. It does say that resources may have to change if this occurs, or some objectives may have to go undone to accommodate some new ones. By engaging in the "catch ball" process during these times, employees and managers can maintain good relationships and contribute to employee satisfaction while accomplishing the goals of the company in a dynamic environment.

Poor Delivery Issues

Managers are people, and they have human flaws. They may feel threatened by their department employees, have little understanding of their detailed work, or have different expectations for employees' goals than those of their employees. So, how do we evaluate employee performance when:

- We are judged by our managers based on their subjective view of good and bad
- We are judged by managers who may be insufficiently trained in completing or delivering an objective performance appraisal
- We are judged by managers who are inclined to avoid conflict or alternatively, those who want to display the power they can exert on your career
- Performance appraisal occurs once a year and is biased toward those activities observed in the last 30-60 days prior to the appraisal and not based on the overall work of employees performed over the entire year period

Managers are often promoted to their leadership positions because they were good performers on the job. However, they lack management skills in organizational dynamics and specifically, motivating and evaluating employees who work for them. They may be great technical specialists, but they may lack the "people" skills necessary to get work done through others.

Some of the skills that managers receive in their college-level course work and/or on-the-job training are in evaluating performance and holding their employees accountable for reaching their goals and adhering to company policies. This is not as easy as it sounds. Achieving goals, performance appraisal, and compensatory reward are tied together.

While many companies claim that employee pay raises are not based on employee performance, this does not ring true. If we are not rewarded for good performance and experience a loss of monetary reward for poor performance, then why should employees perform better than the average? Wouldn't that promote mediocre performance; enough just to get by? In a system where compensation and performance aren't linked, all employees receive the same raises regardless of performance. What motivates an employee to perform better in this system? The prospect of losing their job is supposed to motivate employees to perform better. That is management by fear. As a motivating method, it is at the bottom of the list.

This is not a digression. One of the responsibilities of a manager is to work with employees to mentor them and provide an environment for them to succeed. They provide resources to support the activities of their employees and remove obstacles in their path to success. Poor performance systems directly stand in the way of executing high-performance management methods.

The "Average" Performance Appraisal

Many employees are not led into a discussion about their performance with the goal of evaluating what is going well and jointly plotting a process for improvement. Consider a manager who does not want to disappoint any employee by giving them a poor performance appraisal. Some employees cry when given poor feedback, some become belligerent; some just sit there and refuse to communicate. Especially for a manager who has little or no training in handling these emotional situations, it can be a very uncomfortable meeting for both employee and supervisor. To compensate for that possibility, often a manager will give average performance appraisals to all employees. This results in several benefits for the manager. First, it minimizes negative sentiments in the appraisal meeting. Those who actually perform poorly are pleasantly surprised and let the manager coax them through a quick process. They quickly agree to anything the manager says. Second, difficult salary decisions that strongly differentiate pay raises from the poorest to the best performers are eliminated. If the average pay increase is established by corporate edict as 3.0% overall, the range for employees may be from 2.5% to 3.5%, at most. Thus, when employees compare their performance appraisals and salary increases with each other, no one is that far off the average.

The ones who are hurt by this approach are the hard workers who always meet their goals. They really deserve much higher compensation and sterling performance appraisals, which are indicative of their actual results. But if they receive a disproportionate amount of praise or compensation, when the employees share their reviews with each other, those who didn't fare as well will likely be unhappy. So, this isn't really an option if we adhere to the "average" appraisal process.

The "Truthful" Performance Appraisal

Much harder to do is a performance appraisal based on facts, whatever they are. Naturally, some employees will perform better than others. Those who do a good job should be recognized for that and rewarded appropriately. Those who don't perform well should be counseled on what went wrong and provided help to improve. If an employee fails to improve after several cycles of mentoring, then their fit in the organization may be questioned, and their job may be in jeopardy. Once identified as an employee who routinely fails to meet their goals, employee appraisals may come more frequently than once a year. In fact, quarterly or monthly assessments may be in order to see if real progress is being made in performance.

Doing this is difficult and confrontational even for the best manager even if the message is presented in a caring way, because some people don't take feedback well if it contains any negative information or the suggestion of less than perfect performance. However, this is the fairest way to perform an appraisal. If conducted with sensitivity to the way the information will be received by the employee, it can be a supportive process that lifts the employee to a new level of performance. Knowing what they are doing well, what areas of their performance need improvement, and what resources and support they can get from their managers, many employees will change their behaviors to succeed. It is incumbent on any manager to communicate abundantly.

In addition, the performance appraisal should not uncover new insights that the employee hasn't heard throughout the year. If an employee has the belief that they are doing well in certain areas all through the year, it is unsettling to suddenly hear in an annual performance appraisal that they are mistaken. Hence, feedback on performance should take place all year, even though it is in an informal way. When an employee has completed a project, it is the responsibility of their manager to assess performance, giving praise or suggestions for improvement as often as possible. This leads us to the next point.

Communicate Early and Often

This is one of the most important bits of advice for managers. Since we don't want employees to learn for the first time that they need improvement when they are given their performance appraisal, it is incumbent on the manager to be in constant communication with their employees. This does not mean that every day is a formal appraisal day. However, if an employee misses a deadline, have a constructive conversation with the employee on ways they can recover from the problem. Offering help and advice to the employee will be supportive and non-confrontational. In this scenario, the manager is a resource, not a constant critic. Then, when missing deadlines comes up at the formal appraisal as an area needing improvement, it will come as no surprise.

Linking Compensation to Performance

If there is no correlation between performance and compensation, why would employees work any harder than the lowest performing employee? Well, there are a few reasons, but they miss the point.

One reason employees will perform at their highest level regardless of the level of their pay or their raises is that they want to. They are internally motivated to do a good job and if they believe that they are fairly compensated generally, that is all they need. The satisfaction of doing a good/excellent job is compensation enough. It is a Theory "Y" argument. Another reason for employees to perform at a high level whether or not their compensation reflects this performance is that if they don't, they may fall into a category where their poor performance is worthy of a poor appraisal, and their job may be in jeopardy.

While these are good reasons to expect a disassociation between performance and compensation, it ignores the satisfaction that employees feel when they are recognized for their efforts and success. There is a disconnect when performance isn't correlated highly with compensation, and this is often reflected in poor satisfaction.

Realistic Goals

It is common that employees' performance is judged on criteria over which they have no hands-on control. While it may be argued that all employees contribute to the sales figures and profit of the company, few have the direct ability to affect these figures in their daily activities. Sure, they understand how their performance fits into the profit picture, but there are so many other factors that are not under their direct control, if they do a particularly good job, and another department misses their goals resulting in poor profits, they will not receive their raise or bonus.

That is the first process for goal setting. And, it's likely to be one of the more complicated of our duties.

Assuring that each department and each functional area sets appropriate goals for each individual takes time. As an example, if we have an engineering department that is responsible for new product designs as well as customer support, it probably will be required that engineers have different goals for each of these responsibilities. While we believe that corporate profit is certainly linked to their contribution's success, it is far removed from their daily activities.

One way to look at combining the two is that their daily activity goals will contribute to their salary increases and that corporate profitability will contribute to their bonus. It is fair to assume that a company can't pay out bonuses if they don't make sufficient profit. So, the bonus pool may be determined based on how much money the company makes, and each employees participation in the bonus program is based on their performance and contributions toward the company's profit.

Compensation Policy

Given the complexity of compensation, what would be a fair approach to establishing a compensation policy? We need a process that is easy to understand and places responsibility for compensation on each employee, at least partially on their individual contribution. What are the components of compensation?

Let's look at the elements that comprise the compensation package for our employees. We can list them, excluding such benefits such as vacations, holidays, sick days, bereavement leave, retirement accounts, and healthcare to name a few.

Most common elements of compensation

- Salary/Wages
- Incentive pay
- Commission
- Bonus

Now let's look at them one at a time to break-out the most realistic approach for setting compensation in each of these areas.

Salary/Wages

What is a fair wage? In most cases it is the price an employer must pay to hire competent workers in each functional area, and in each geographic area. If there are lots of prospective employees willing and competent to work for $11.00 per hour, no company would be justified in paying $12.00 per hour for their work. This model assumes that there is an ample supply of workers so that even a new company looking for workers won't have to poach workers from other employers by offering higher than market wages.

This is the same argument whether we are looking at hourly or salaried employees. If an Operations Manager is willing to work for $50,000 per year in your locale, then paying more is a questionable tactic. Most businesses would perceive this as wasteful and they spend quite a bit of time and money to benchmark their wage structure against industry averages in their community for similar job classifications.

Incentive Pay

Incentive pay is intended to motivate employees to contribute at a high performance level. It may be used to distinguish between high performers and those who don't achieve at the same level. As an example, if we have two employees in a department with the same responsibilities and one does the job, but the other performs the job better, their incentive pay would reflect this difference. How would this work, objectively?

Let's say that these two employees, A and B both have the same job descriptions and they are both in the same service area. They are judged by the number of customers they help each month and the level of customer satisfaction directly attributable to their individual customer support. Employee A routinely registers higher metrics in both areas, when Employee B does not receive such high metrics regularly. Therefore, employee A should receive higher incentive compensation than employee B. This same comparison would also be used to set these employee's raises in salary, but is in addition to the incentive pay differential.

Commission

Commission is a form of incentive pay that is directly attributable to a pre-determined pay-for-performance plan. This is most prevalent in sales roles. In its purest form, some jobs are paid on a straight commission basis. If you sell something at a certain price, you get a percentage of the sale amount or a percentage of the profit directly attributable to that sale.. If you don't sell anything, you don't get paid anything. There are many different combinations of salary and commission compensation plans.

Bonus

We can provide additional compensation for employees across the board when the company does well. This is in recognition of the contribution that all employees make to the company's success. So, if the company has a sliding scale, it might look like this, for example:

Company Profit	Bonus as a Percent of Base Salary
$1,000,000	0%
$1,000,001 – $1,200,000	4%
$1,200,001–$1,400,000	8%
$1,400,001 and above	10%

Those Other Elements of Compensation

The various other elements of compensation can really add up. Employees ignore them at their peril. I know many workers who have given up their jobs and taken work with another company for a raise of 50 cents an hour, only to lose important benefits that more than compensate for that wage increase. For instance:

- Vacation pay: The average work year is about 2000 hours (40 hours a week times 50 weeks a year). Therefore, each vacation day (8 hours of paid time off) is the equivalent of 0.4% of your pay each year.
- Holidays: Using the same calculation as vacation days, each additional holiday offered by the company or declined by company policy on the new job is 0.4% of your pay each year.
- Sick days: Each sick day is also worth 0.4% of your pay each year.
- Bereavement time off: Each day of paid bereavement is also worth 0.4% of your pay each year.
- Professional development: A company might pay for you to attend conferences, receive continuing education units to maintain certifications or professional licenses, take in-service courses or training, or pay tuition reimbursement for college courses.
- 401k company match: There is substantial variability in the policies that companies have in matching employee contributions to their retirement funds. With the steady elimination of defined pension plans, these differences are very important. If a company will match the first 5% of contributions to your 401k account, that is like receiving a 5% raise just because you decided to save money to fund your retirement.
- Healthcare contributions: The topic of healthcare coverage is more complicated because it has (at least) two dimensions. The first dimension is the coverage of the plan versus your current plan. Some

plans may not cover a needed medical treatment that another one will. Some have different deductibles or co-payment requirements. However, in addition to this, different companies require different amounts of contributions on the part of the employee. Say a policy costs $10,000 per year and Company A requires a 20% contribution from the employee. The employee pays $2000.00, or $38.46 per week in contributions to the plan. In this case, the company pays $153.85 per week to subsidize that employee's plan. Say Company B requires a 30% contribution on the part of the employee. Now the employee pays $57.69 per week and the company pays $134.61 per week. Your additional $1000 per year contribution is a significant reduction in your take home pay.

- Conveniences: Several companies, especially those that make it to the top 100 companies to work for in the nation (or your state) provide babysitting service on-site, dry cleaning pick up, car washes, sports leagues, subsidized cafeteria services, fitness memberships, and a host of other convenience items to employees. One company will permit employees to have their pets accompany them to work and they accommodate the pets' needs in the workspace and on the grounds of the facility.

Compensation Ladders

Problems occur when we put in place compensation plans that specify managers must be the highest paid employees at the company. This shouldn't be the case in many companies. Here is an example. When a company employs highly skilled and/or highly educated employees, a manager might not be the senior person in the department. Consider an engineer with 25 years of experience who has worked their way up from Jr. Engineer to Sr. Engineer and then to Engineering Specialist. This is the job that this employee wants. They may have no interest in the management of an Engineering Department.

Now, contrast that to a first-time manager in the Engineering Department who is being given their first supervisory job. This department needs engineering specialists to do the day-to-day work. It is possible that the company might benefit from the Engineering Specialist being paid more than the department manager in the Engineering Department.

If we consider a simple example of this with three different job categories, it might look like this:

Compensation Comparison for Three Different Job Categories			
Compensation (Base)	Administration Ladder	Technical/Professional Ladder	Management Ladder
Above 180,000			COO/CEO/President
180,000			Executive Vice President
160,000			Senior Vice President
140,000			Vice President
120,000		Program Manager	
100,000		Principal Engineer/ Project Manager	Division Manager
80,000		Senior Engineer/ Statistician	Unit Manager
60,000	Executive Assistant	Senior Engineer/CPA	Department Manager
40,000	Senior Admin. Assistant	Engineer/ Financial Analyst	
20,000	Admin. Assistant		
10,000			

In this simple case, an Executive Assistant might make more money than an entry level engineer, and a Project Manager might make more money than a Department or Unit Manager. This is not to say that an Executive Vice President of a company might not make much more money than $180,000. It is a scale that communicates the midpoint of a range of salaries indicating that managers might have some very senior contributors on their staff who are highly compensated, in fact, making more in base salary than their department manager.

Not dealing with this simple process is one way a company will skew salary scales and push those on the management ladder significantly ahead of technical specialists who will feel held back because their contribution isn't as valued as those of the "managers". By the same argument, managers want to be compensated for the skills they have in coordinating the efforts of all their employees and one way to have (and convey) that sense of position is to enjoy the biggest salary in the department. My view is that these managers should get over the perception that they are only viewed as important as the size of their compensation.

CHAPTER 9: CONTINUOUS IMPROVEMENT PROCESS

"Management is about arranging and telling. Leadership is about nurturing and enhancing." Thomas J. Peters

Continual Improvement

Staying the same is not an option. Those who rest on their past performance and fail to improve will fall behind because maintaining the status quo lets your competitors race ahead. By having a strategy to stay the same, you end up lagging the field. The world advances, and each of us must advance just to keep current with the rest of our competitors. Success comes only to those who improve more than the others in a competitive environment.

Continual improvement is a scientific method intended to measure the current state of performance, in our case employee engagement, and then set a goal for increasing the value of engagement over time. This is also called the kaizen approach, which is a Japanese term for continuous (or continual) improvement accomplished in many small steps. It is characterized by incremental gains (evolutionary improvement) and not giant leaps (revolutionary changes). Kaizen is a process within the organizational system that must be documented and integrated into the daily work structure with review cycles and project evaluations.

In manufacturing environments this is often referred to as "Quality Circles". Employees are trained to meet and continuously improve the manufacturing process, with an understanding that a change in one department may have consequences (both intended and unintended) in other departments. So, teams are established with enough coverage in production, accounting, purchasing, and quality control that the impact of a change in one department can be analyzed for its potential systems impact to reduce the possibility of fixing one problem but causing another one somewhere else.

There is confusion in the literature about whether the process is called *continuous* improvement or *continual* improvement. This is more of an academic issue than a practical one. Many writers use the terms interchangeably with the clear preference being continuous. However, continuous is often given a mathematical interpretation meaning that there are no discontinuities in the graph of the time series, while continual is considered to be improvement based on discrete steps (jumps) moving performance from one level to another instantaneously, or over a very short timeframe. In reality, when we change a process and enjoy an improvement in performance, one day we did it the old way and the next day we do it the new way, so increases in performance really are continual since they occur in discrete steps.

The following graph shows the distinction between continuous and continual improvement processes. It is clear that we typically have continual process improvement when we work on our quality circles projects.

Continuous vs. Continual Improvement

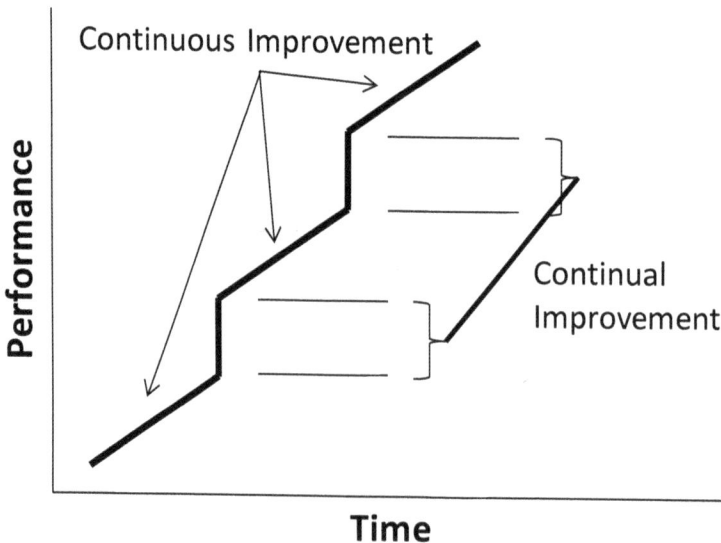

The Challenge

Improvement comes from planning, not usually by virtue of an accident. Just because we had a plan to improve employee satisfaction last year and we reached our goal doesn't mean that the job is over. Without a strategy to continue developing projects for employee satisfaction improvement, we will likely lose ground. Motivational theory tells us that once an improvement in satisfaction is achieved by engaging in a new process for employees, it is motivational for a short time. Then, it is expected and while losing the improvement will shift satisfaction lower, maintaining it will not continue to increase satisfaction and maintenance of the improvement over several years, with no other offsetting improvements will result in a slide-back of satisfaction.

Other issues that carried less importance to satisfaction will become more important and need to be addressed for satisfaction to move to higher levels. I consulted for a company that had significant issues with their treatment by management. In a survey of broad-based questions, this was consistent among all employee groups. The company took action to correct this issue and when I conducted the survey the following year the number one issue was the cleanliness of the bathrooms. Not a single mention of management mistreatment was made. In write-in comments many employees made unsolicited statements about the improvement in management treatment.

If a process is important to us, it should be in the plan every year. I worked for a company that had an objective to decrease the cost of its highest volume product by $5.00 each year. It was a hugely successful annual program that concentrated a team's efforts on vendors, designers, and engineers to improve the quality and decrease the cost of the product each year. It is this concerted effort that displays the importance of the project to the company. It also highlights the meaning of continual improvement in an organization. The successful achievement of a goal is not the end of the process. Continual improvement is a never-ending journey that is part of the strategic and operating plans every year. Employee satisfaction should fall under this process of annual measurement and improvement.

The Problem

The methods of problem-solving can be applied to any opportunity. In our context we are discussing employee satisfaction, so let's stick with this concept. When we want to improve employee satisfaction/loyalty/engagement we should start with a process to determine what the employees want, then compare these suggestions to our corporate mission and find which employee suggestions intersect, or at least don't conflict with our mission. It is those suggestions that we want to concentrate on for improvement. It is not strange for employees to say that their work lives would be improved if the company would make some changes to better satisfy the company's customers. But, we would never know unless we asked. This is the reason why we conduct employee satisfaction surveys every year. It jump-starts the improvement process and gives us actionable items on which to concentrate our efforts.

The System

As we discuss in other chapters, unless we can show that there is a systematic approach to implementing a process, it is uncertain that any gains we enjoy actually came from a defined plan or are instead the result of serendipity. When an auditor reviews your company's results, it helps if the company can point to a project that was conducted with the goal of achieving that result, and the project was successful. Otherwise, there is no explanation for the results, so the company has a hard time justifying that the benefits are sustainable. In other words, if your projections are for increasing performance and there is no reason given for why that is likely to occur, the increases enjoyed so far may be considered nothing more than statistical variation. Increases (or decreases) are not justified unless there is a causative reason for their occurrence. A closed system that might define a process improvement would be:

Strategic plan: Improving employee satisfaction from 89% to 91% in the next 12 months

Operating plan:

- Conduct employee satisfaction survey and analyze results
- Meet with employees to discuss survey results
- Request feedback from employees on ways to improve satisfaction
- Review comments with Operating Committee
- Choose most likely methods that fit with corporate objectives
- Implement approved employee ideas
- Poll employees on the success of the new initiatives
- Continue the initiatives or modify as necessary
- Conduct annual employee satisfaction survey to confirm meeting the strategic goal of 91% employee satisfaction

Now, at the end of the year when employee satisfaction is reported, any improvement can be linked to the specific project conducted throughout the year and that project should be credited as the cause of the improvement.

The Process

Continual improvement starts with an understanding of the process. Improvement will never occur unless there is a mandate to formally work on it. This may start with the strategic plan.

The process is one of:

- Brainstorming
- Training
- Teamwork
- Problem-solving
- Confirmation
- Continual Improvement

We can consider this process to be the structure of a problem-solving approach. Once we train employees on this way of approaching problems, we can begin to form teams to solve those problems.

The PDCA Cycle

Here is the graphic for the Plan – Do – Check – Act cycle:

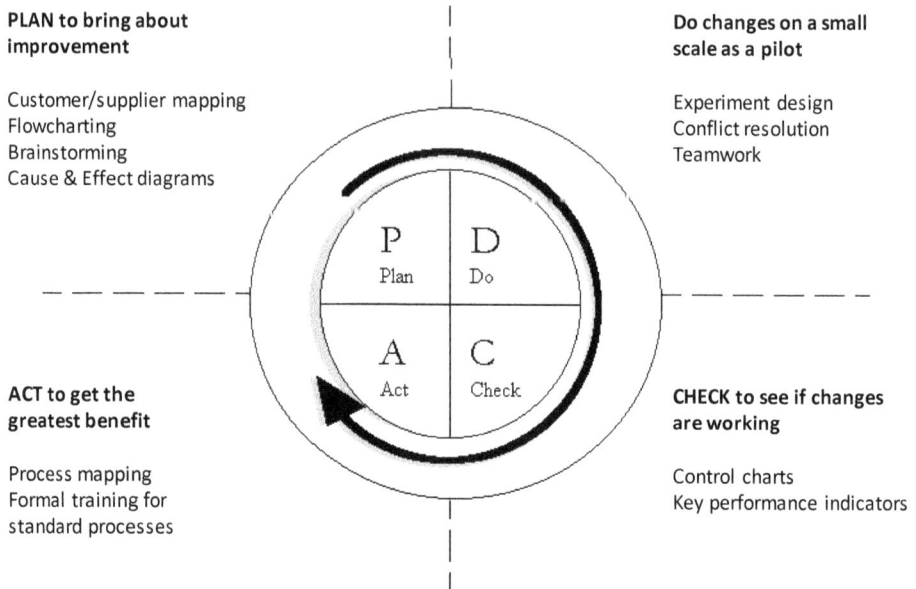

PLAN to bring about improvement

Customer/supplier mapping
Flowcharting
Brainstorming
Cause & Effect diagrams

Do changes on a small scale as a pilot

Experiment design
Conflict resolution
Teamwork

P — Plan

D — Do

A — Act

C — Check

ACT to get the greatest benefit

Process mapping
Formal training for standard processes

CHECK to see if changes are working

Control charts
Key performance indicators

This is essentially the scientific method which is a systematic way to address problem solving. The first step is the definition of the problem, which requires us to look into the problem statement. Let's say that employees are unhappy with the cafeteria. They rate the cafeteria 5 on a scale of 1 to 10, where 10 is a rating of "highly satisfied". So, we know that there is something wrong with the cafeteria. That is a symptom of the problem, but what is the cause of the problem? What should we implement to improve employee satisfaction with the cafeteria?

That takes us to the Plan stage of PDCA. We need to brainstorm about likely reasons for dissatisfaction with the cafeteria.

Brainstorming:

In the Plan stage, one of the activities is getting the team to propose all the possible reasons (underlying, or root causes) that employees don't like the cafeteria. We can use a fishbone diagram, sometimes referred to as a cause-and-effect diagram to list the potential causes of dissatisfaction with the cafeteria.

This is a general form of the fishbone diagram. The problem is the effect, and it is caused by many potential underlying issues with equipment, process, people, materials, environment, and management. We are looking for the root cause of the problem. What underlies the issue? What can we find that is actionable. Knowing that the cafeteria is problematic is important, but this information is insufficient to generate a plan to fix it.

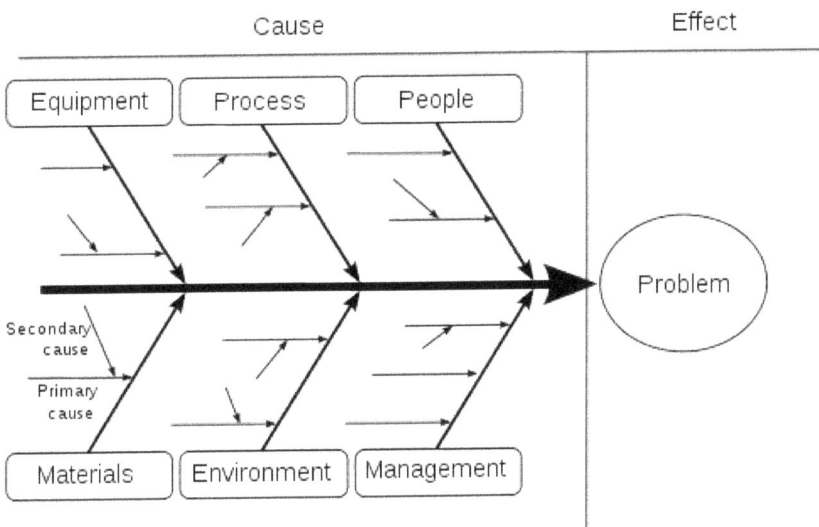

In our cafeteria case, we can meet with our group and brainstorm the causes of dissatisfaction:

- Equipment: Is the toaster broken? Is the cooler too small and certain menu items are constantly running out?
- Process: Are there too few checkout lines causing delays? Too few griddles slowing down food service? Are there too few hours of operation?
- People: Are the food preparers surly? Do the checkout clerks make mistakes constantly?
- Materials: Does the food taste bad? Are the napkins rough?

- Environment: Are the chairs uncomfortable? Is the cafeteria always cold in winter and too hot in the summer?
- Management: Is the manager non-responsive or often absent?
- Training: Training is in the Do portion of the cycle. Like education, training is a challenge because we need to change the way people think and behave if we are to make improvement.

Humans inherently resist change, and therefore, it is hard to get people to open their minds to new ways of doing things. We tend to have opinions about life events that are based on prior beliefs or experience (whether those prior beliefs are based on factual information or not) and they are continuously reinforced by our selective processing of new information. It is called cognitive dissonance.

Essentially, when we have a belief and we hear or see information that confirms our belief, we accept that information as true. However, when we encounter information that is opposite to our belief, we ignore it and justify that by thinking the new information must be wrong. We become uncomfortable having conflicting cognitions in our minds simultaneously. Hearing or seeing new information that conflicts with our prior beliefs creates dissonance, which is an uncomfortable feeling that we could be wrong. It sets up a battle in our mind that we are unsure what to believe and we are driven to resolve the dissonance and create a consistent belief system in our mind. We then try to create consonance, or a relieved feeling that we know what is right, and we do this by ignoring the new facts (information) and relying on our prior knowledge.

When we have a prior belief that a process is good, or has been working for a long time, we become conflicted when we hear that a change is required. Our first thought is to convince others that no change is required. "We tried that before and it didn't work", "I see a problem with that new proposal", or "What's wrong with the way we are doing things?" are ways to fend off change. However, when we are misinformed in our prior knowledge, we are not thinking in a progressive way, or we haven't considered the benefits of improvement, then we are closing our minds to beneficial change. So the process of learning is a process of breaking our prior beliefs and accepting new information that resets our belief system. We must be open to that change.

Brainstorming is the first step in expanding our minds to new ideas. So, part of training is to help the team understand that our prior beliefs may not be accurate or progressive enough, and we need to embrace the possibility of change.

Employees are not generally experts in problem-solving methodologies or working effectively in teams. Neither are they consciously aware of the difficulty inherent in driving change in an organization, either from the operational aspects to the human development aspects. If a dedicated program of improvement is to be implemented, then those employees who are chosen to be on the team should receive training in these areas.

Teamwork:

Teamwork is also in the Do portion of the PDCA cycle. This is where we form teams and we go through the Forming, Storming, Norming, and Performing process of team building, including skills of working on teams as a functional member and getting along with others. It involves conflict resolution and leadership skills.

Tuchman (1965) introduced this model of group dynamics to describe the phases required for team development, and it is still in use today.

	Knowledge Is Hidden	Knowledge Creation	
Trust Unknown	Forming	Performing	Synergizes
Distrust	Storming	Norming	Collaborates
	Knowledge Hoarding	Knowledge Sharing	

When we first form a team, it is made up of individuals, each of whom has talents necessary to solve the problem (symptom) we have identified. We are still in the Do phase, and in this stage it is recognized that one person doesn't have the skills to solve the problem alone; we need a team with a wide array of knowledge to handle complex issues.

In the Forming stage, we may be working with people we have never met before and we don't know their ability to work on a team, so our level of trust in them is low and each of us has specialty knowledge unknown to the rest of the team. [In cases where we have worked with one of more members of the team on prior projects, this Forming process is substantially shortened.]

Looking forward, the goal is to have a fully functioning team where they are creating knowledge unique to the problem to be solved and each member of the team can rely on every other member to contribute strongly to the team's efforts. We can count on their ability, attention to detail, ability to work cooperatively on the team without regard to who gets the credit, and the timeliness of their work.

However, before we get there, we have to get through the Storming stage. Some team members never make it through this stage. It is here that the team leader must decide whether the members who were originally selected for the team will acclimate to a team environment. This is cut-time.

Some people have a tough time giving up on the status quo. They have internal conflicts about change and can't embrace the process of change from a proactive stance. They won't be contributors to the team's activities; they will be obstacles.

Some people have difficulty accepting the skills and authority of other team members. For instance, they might argue that the accountant isn't considering costs properly, or that the views of the Marketing Department don't carry the weight of other Departments' needs.

Some people are uncomfortable working with others. They prefer being individual contributors and are intimidated by the complexity of large projects and many opinions being voiced. They are lost in a fast-paced environment and find it difficult, if not impossible to keep up.

Whatever the reason, one or more members may be weeded out as the team begins to work together. There is still some distrust and team members are carving out their turf. They each want to be known as the expert in their particular specialty. However, they still haven't begun working on the problem. The ground rules are made clear, the process is described, and the issue is developed. The team is hesitating, but they are starting to see where they fit in the mix.

Problem-Solving:

By the time we get to the Problem-Solving stage, the team is working together cooperatively. This is still in the Do part of the process. Now we can apply those problem-solving techniques we were taught in the training sessions and engage in brainstorming and trusting the input from others on the team. We are in the Norming stage. This is where the work of the team is done.

- The underlying causes are listed and potential solutions are discussed.
- The most promising solutions are analyzed for their business implications.
- Ways to implement solutions and prove the efficacy of changes are established.
- The most likely solution candidates to reach our goals are chosen and a method of implementation is selected.
- Plans are put in place, all involved employees are informed of the proposed changes, documentation is prepared and employees are trained in the new process.
- Then, changes are introduced to solve the problem.

The creative part of the process is in problem-solving. It requires the most technical ability and the most analysis, since we are often choosing between alternative solutions and the team must evaluate the changes from a systems perspective to avoid unintended consequences in other parts of the company's operations. Financial implications must be considered to see if the solution(s) are financially attractive.

At this point we are ready to run a pilot test to evaluate the efficacy of the proposed solution.

Confirmation:

Confirmation occurs in the Check and Act stages. We want hard evidence that what we proposed will achieve the goals originally set for the project in a full roll-out. Does the solution resolve the problem? If it does, the team will take us to the Act stage and engage full documentation and implementation of the changes throughout the organization. If not, we will go back to our team for a review of the failed results and another round of problem-solving. If the team believes that another solution option already identified in the last round (but not chosen for implementation) is worth a try, it should be recommended for the next pilot. However, if the remaining options that were identified previously appear unworthy of a pilot, the team will take the process back to brainstorming and begin again.

Another part of confirmation is the process of maintaining the gains. It is natural for any change in a process to experience retrogression, or a back-sliding into the old ways of doing things. Despite the changes that we make in documentation and operational flow, and the training we provide to employees in the new process, people are likely to resist change and go back to the old familiar processes instead. By constantly monitoring and auditing the operation and its results, we can identify when the changes aren't being followed and more training and/or reinforcement is required. This is an important part of any change if we want it to be durable. Auditing can help us discover any change in the operation that deviates from the new documented process, and get us back on track.

Continual Improvement:

Once we have discovered a weakness in our organization, it is naive to think that it can fix all our issues. Our problem-solving exercise has proven that we can make improvement, but is one round enough, or should we set continual improvement goals each planning period to beat the best competition we have (our benchmark?) This is a continuous process because we can only work on one or a few projects in any one planning period. Those that we choose not to work on will be eliminated from consideration or held for future planning periods giving us fertile ground to continuously improve satisfaction.

Employee satisfaction is not a single number; it is a series of numbers that represent how employees feel every day, every week, or month, or year. And, since things change in organizations on a daily basis, you can expect people's feelings to change in response to the stimulus of daily life. We have employees leaving voluntarily or some employees are dismissed. These folks have friends in the organization and those who remain may be affected by this change in workplace environment. Benefits change, profit-sharing changes year to year, job responsibilities change, your boss may change and you might like the change or not like the way the new boss interacts with employees. Your interactions with other departments may get better or worse. The workplace is a dynamic environment and each of these factors affect how we feel about our jobs and how well we are engaged with our employer.

It is not advised that we poll our employees about their level of satisfaction more than once a year. However, if we polled them weekly, we would see some dramatic variations in satisfaction levels as the employees go through the weekly changes in personnel, policy, or environment. Over the course of a year these shocks tend to fade in our memory and year-over-year employee satisfaction numbers are a reliable way to measure our progress. The criticism of polling employees at all centers on the bad luck of conducting the survey just after a major upset, such as a change in the benefit plan that is not popular with employees. Obviously, we will be polling our employees at a low point in satisfaction, and this will bias our results.

This is known as the halo or horns effect. When something happens that is beneficial to employees in the weeks just prior to conducting the survey, they tend to bias employee responses in the survey toward higher levels of satisfaction regardless of their views averaged over the entire year. This is the halo effect. It is also common in performance appraisals, where an employee has a great success just prior to the formal performance appraisal process. Their rating is often higher because of the glow surrounding their performance most recently. The horns effect is just the opposite. Something negative happens in the organization just prior to the satisfaction survey and it biases employee responses to the lower levels of satisfaction even though their average over the year would have been higher if it weren't for this recent occurrence.

The counterpoint argument is that we can never guarantee a date to conduct the survey that is sufficiently removed in time from a change in the organization not to encounter this phenomenon. If we waited for that perfect time to occur, we may never conduct a survey. So, we instruct employees to ignore any current events and focus on the entire year instead. We believe that these annual surveys will show trends that are meaningful and will help us renew the organization in ways that are most beneficial to employees and the company. We tell the survey respondents that if they have any comments about recent events, these should be included in the write-in section of the survey.

Once we analyze our survey results, we want to understand the impact of our satisfaction metrics and determine whether we have achieved our goal of improving satisfaction, and find a way to communicate the results to our employees. This will take an analysis tool and usually some graphical way to display the outcome of the study. Run Charts can be a very useful device in this regard.

Run Charts

A method we can use to display our survey results is called a Run Chart. This is a simple way to graphically show the values of satisfaction over time. We can also see how we are trending with our results. Here is an example of a fictitious Run Chart:

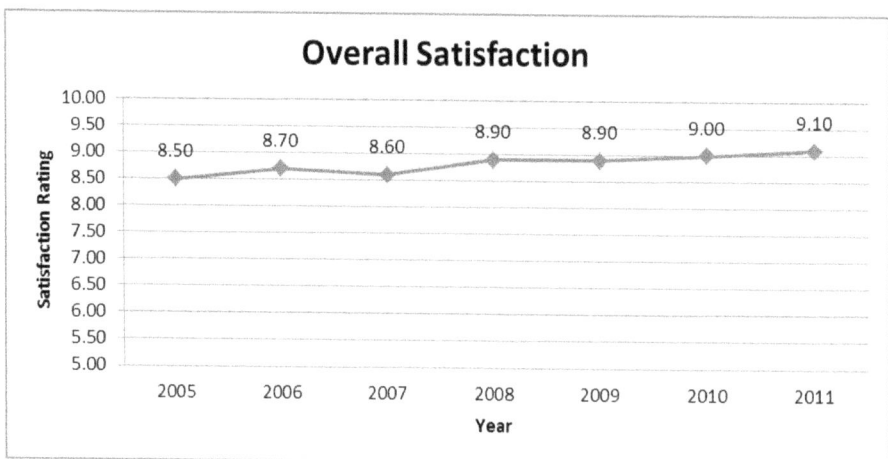

In this chart, we notice that in 2007 there was a decline in overall satisfaction. However, this is a natural part of surveying. The company may have experienced a negative shock that impacted employees with the result that satisfaction declined. However, when we review satisfaction, we want to look at the long term, and we can see that there is increasing satisfaction in this fictitious company.

Also, the scale has been selected with a minimum of 5.0 rather than 0.0. Using the scaling to highlight trend lines is a common way to visually create a dramatic conclusion. For instance, if we were to use a minimum of 8.0 on the graph, the satisfaction scores would look like this:

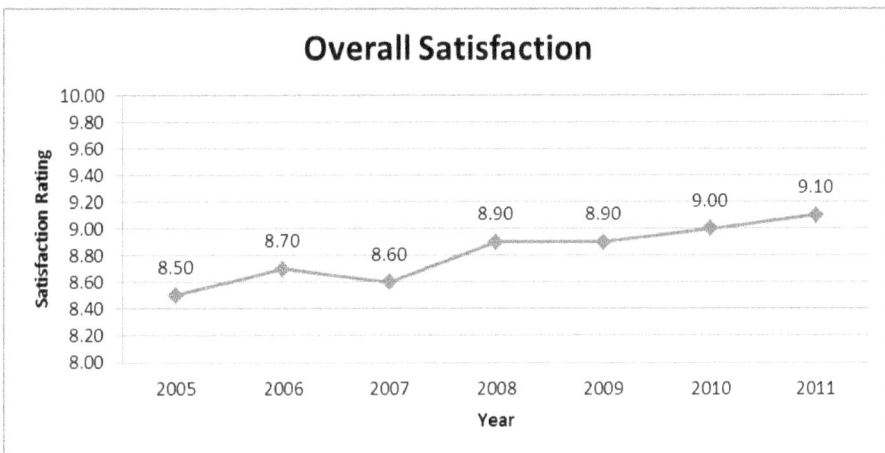

Overall Satisfaction

What appeared to be a flatter improvement in satisfaction now appears to be much more sloped, conveying a feeling of more rapid improvement in satisfaction. Don't be fooled by scaling tricks to prove a point. The numbers are identical in these two graphs, but the minimum value is altered to make it appear as if the numbers are increasing more rapidly.

Alternatively, since the low point of the scale is arbitrarily set, we might fix it at 0.0 and the satisfaction graph would appear to be much flatter, visually suggesting that not much progress has been made over the last 6 years since our baseline in 2005. The only way to mathematically evaluate whether there is improvement, and how much confidence we have in the numbers is to perform an analysis of the data to evaluate any trends that are justified by a statistical analysis.

Generally, in a continual improvement model, we want to see a trend that is increasing in time.

A Run Chart is a mechanism to display numerical values and how they change over time. The trend should not be construed as a prediction. It is often inappropriate to project the line into future time periods. It is merely a way to show what has happened, not what to expect in the future. Employee satisfaction is based on continuous actions on the part of the organization to measure and impact satisfaction. A positive trend line indicates that what the company has done is working. It is a testament to the success of the project. However, it is not true that if the company stops the process of working on continual improvement, we will still enjoy upward trending results into the future. Nor is it prudent to predict future results. We should set future goals and those activities that we believe can achieve the goals, but then conduct satisfaction surveys to confirm satisfaction results after the improvement process has had a chance to be implemented.

Regressions

Regressions (trend lines) may be used in the analysis of time series data. It is tempting to simply extrapolate a linear trend to predict the dependent variable into future time periods and textbooks show how to do this. But, that is the same as using a crystal ball to calculate the future increase in satisfaction without any knowledge of the actions management will take to effect employee satisfaction. And, since the actions are predecessor events to the measurement, we believe that they are causative, and therefore important to know before we predict future satisfaction.

As an analysis tool for past performance, we want to determine our confidence level that satisfaction has improved. Can we say categorically that the improvement we are witnessing is based on a statistically significant increase, or is the data more representative of random variation with no real trend at all?

One way to analyze the data is to perform a regression on the values to see if there is a reason for us to have a slope in the graph. The only reason to have a regression line is to explain a phenomenon that a simple average can't explain in its entirety. For instance, in the satisfaction data from 2005 through 2011, the average satisfaction rating is 8.8. But by looking at the plot of the data, there is something else we can learn if we break out the time element of the series and look at the trend. It appears to be going up over time. This information is quite valuable to us since it signals that something is probably happening to cause increasing satisfaction. This causal effect should be credited to actions we have taken to improve satisfaction, and not just random variation.

Now that we have postulated that the data appear to be increasing, and there is additional value to analyzing the series because it may indicate a positive trend, we need to find a way to confirm statistically that it is likely that the trend is meaningful and not just random variation. We can do this by creating a regression of the data and interpreting the output from the regression. This plot shows the linear regression for the data. The diamonds are the original data and the boxes are the overlaid points on the regression line that correspond to the regression equation that represents the predicted line.

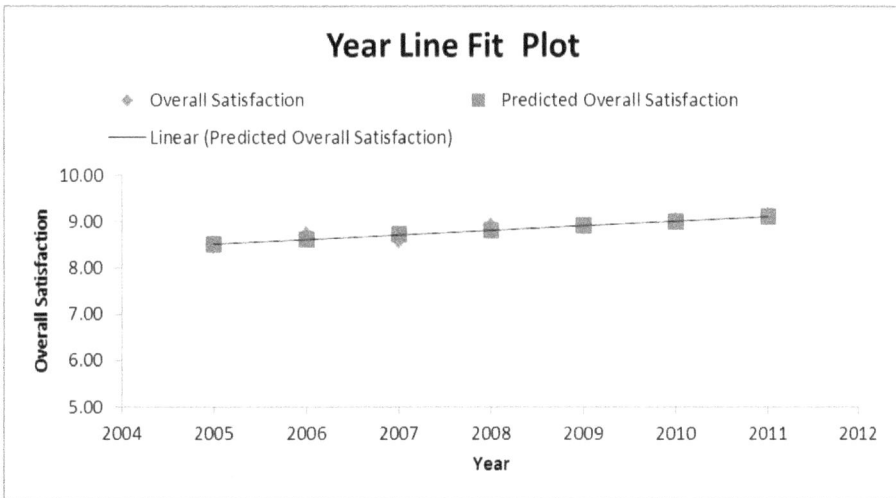

While it appears that there is a clear upward trend, and the satisfaction data appear to be linearly increasing with time, we also have some output from the regression to help us determine the statistical significance of the trend line. When we perform a regression one of the choices we have to make is the confidence level we want in any conclusions drawn from the data. The default confidence level in Excel regressions is 95% confidence. We have the ability to change that level, but failing to choose some other level of confidence, 95% is used in all calculations. Some of the tabular output is shown here:

SUMMARY OUTPUT

Regression Statistics	
Multiple R	0.949856685
R Square	0.902227723
Adjusted R Square	0.882673267
Standard Error	0.075118953
Observations	7

ANOVA

	df	SS	MS	F	Significance F
Regression	1	0.260357143	0.260357	46.13924	0.001052493
Residual	5	0.028214286	0.005643		
Total	6	0.288571429			

	Coefficients	Standard Error	t Stat	P-value
Intercept	-184.814286	28.50587891	-6.48337	0.001302
Year	0.096428571	0.014196148	6.792587	0.001052

The most important data from the regression output have been highlighted.

The R Squared value is the coefficient of determination. In this case its value is 0.902, or 90.2%. The coefficient of determination is the proportion of variation in satisfaction that is explained by the passage of time. It has a relatively high value which means that only 9.8% of the variation in satisfaction may be due to factors that can't be explained simply by the causal effects that impact satisfaction over time.

The next output factor is the significance F value, which is the confidence level we have in declaring the regression to be representative of the data. In other words, if the regression equation does not add to our understanding of the data, we would conclude that the regression line does not represent the data well and there is no need for the slope. A simple average alone is all that is needed to explain the data. The smaller the significance F value, the more confidence we have that the equation is needed to provide a better explanation of the data than a simple average of the individual values. The test of significance is 1.0 minus the confidence interval that we want. If we assume that we want to be 95% certain of our conclusions, then any significance F value lower than 0.05 demonstrates at least a 95% confidence level that there is significance in the slope to the data, and we have more information about the trend than can be explained with a simple average alone. In this case, the significance $F = 0.00105$, which is much less than 0.05, giving us high confidence that there is statistical significance for the slope not to be zero, and to conclude that the slope of the line is meaningful and adds to our understanding of the data.

There are two coefficients in the output data. One is the Intercept, which is the location that the regression line would cross the satisfaction axis at a year of zero. In our case, this value is totally meaningless. The other coefficient is the slope coefficient, which is a value of 0.0964 for this data, which means that satisfaction has increased by 0.0964 each year, or rounded out to approximately 0.1 each year. It is the slope of the regression line. We started with a satisfaction score of 8.5, and 6 years later we have a score of 8.5 + 6 x 0.1 = 9.1, which matches the regression equation as well as the data.

The p-values tell us the confidence level of the coefficients in the regression equation. The most important one is the value of 0.001052 for the slope coefficient. Any time the p-value is lower than our acceptable error value (in this case 0.05, or 5%), we have better than 95% confidence in the coefficient. A regression equation is the best fit of a line to the data, but that doesn't mean it is a good fit. The Excel output gives us information for us to evaluate the statistical evidence for the goodness of fit [of the data to the regression equation.] In this case, the p-values are much lower than 0.05, and that means we have excellent confidence in the slope value, or that satisfaction has increased by 0.1 each year.

Once this analysis is complete we can say that we have statistical evidence that satisfaction has improved over the 6 years in our analysis, and that we have confidence in the rate of improvement as represented by the regression data. Lest we forget, the original goal of our continual improvement program was to reinvent the process each year to find ways to increase satisfaction in the workforce. This analysis is intended to prove that there is statistical significance in our attestation that satisfaction has indeed improved.

In 2012, we would simply add the survey value to the data set to show the expanded trend line and recalculate the regression equation to see if there was a change in the slope or a change in the confidence level of the regression.

Postscript

As evidenced by the arguments in this book, there are responsibilities for employees and employers if we want to achieve high levels of employee satisfaction. The environment set by the company in its policies and practices is a major factor in promoting a daily feeling in employees that they want to "go to work." The employee's attitudes and behaviors also contribute to their own happiness on the job. The interface is in things like training and development, succession and career planning, and open communication. These provide the link that matches employee and employer needs to create a harmonious workplace where there is respect for everyone's efforts and a genuine desire to get the business of the business accomplished in the most efficient way. The company benefits and the employees are rewarded for their good work and feel gratified by a job well done. It all is directed by LEADERSHIP. It is more than words.

According to a Chinese Proverb,

"Not the cry, but the flight of the wild duck, leads the flock to fly and follow."

Some companies have accomplished that goal. It can be done.

INDEX